(ex·ploring)

1. Investigating in a systematic way: examining. 2. Searching into or ranging over for the purpose of discovery.

Getting Started with

Microsoft®
Windows® 10

(ex·ploring)

SERIES

1. Investigating in a systematic way: examining. 2. Searching into or ranging over for the purpose of discovery.

Getting Started with

Microsoft®
Windows® 10

Mary Anne Poatsy

Series Created by Dr. Robert T. Grauer

PEARSON

Boston   Columbus   Indianapolis   New York   San Francisco
Amsterdam   Cape Town   Dubai   London   Madrid   Milan   Munich   Paris   Montréal   Toronto
Delhi   Mexico City   São Paulo   Sydney   Hong Kong   Seoul   Singapore   Taipei   Tokyo

Vice President of Career Skills: Andrew Gilfillan
Senior Editor: Samantha Lewis
Team Lead, Project Management: Laura Burgess
Project Manager: Laura Karahalis
Program Manager: Emily Biberger
Development Editor: Barbara Stover
Editorial Assistant: Michael Campbell
Director of Product Marketing: Maggie Waples
Director of Field Marketing: Leigh Ann Sims
Product Marketing Manager: Kaylee Carlson
Field Marketing Managers: Molly Schmidt & Joanna Sabella
Marketing Coordinator: Susan Osterlitz
Senior Operations Specialist: Diane Peirano
Senior Art Director: Diane Ernsberger
Interior and Cover Design: Diane Ernsberger
Cover Photo: Courtesy of Shutterstock® Images
Associate Director of Design: Blair Brown
Senior Product Strategy Manager: Eric Hakanson
Product Manager, MyITLab: Zachary Alexander
Media Producer, MyITLab: Jaimie Noy
Digital Project Manager, MyITLab: Becca Lowe
Media Project Manager, Production: John Cassar
Full-Service Project Management: Jenna Vittorioso, Lumina Datamatics, Inc.
Composition: Lumina Datamatics, Inc.
Efficacy Curriculum Manager: Jessica Sieminski

Credits and acknowledgments borrowed from other sources and reproduced, with permission, in this textbook appear on the appropriate page within text.

Microsoft and/or its respective suppliers make no representations about the suitability of the information contained in the documents and related graphics published as part of the services for any purpose. All such documents and related graphics are provided "as is" without warranty of any kind. Microsoft and/or its respective suppliers hereby disclaim all warranties and conditions with regard to this information, including all warranties and conditions of merchantability, whether express, implied or statutory, fitness for a particular purpose, title and non-infringement. In no event shall Microsoft and/or its respective suppliers be liable for any special, indirect or consequential damages or any damages whatsoever resulting from loss of use, data or profits, whether in an action of contract, negligence or other tortious action, arising out of or in connection with the use or performance of information available from the services.

The documents and related graphics contained herein could include technical inaccuracies or typographical errors. Changes are periodically added to the information herein. Microsoft and/or its respective suppliers may make improvements and/or changes in the product(s) and/or the program(s) described herein at any time. Partial screen shots may be viewed in full within the software version specified.

Microsoft® and Windows® are registered trademarks of the Microsoft Corporation in the U.S.A. and other countries. This book is not sponsored or endorsed by or affiliated with the Microsoft Corporation.

Library of Congress Control Number: 2015947643

10 9 8 7 6 5 4 3 2 1

ISBN-10:   0-13-440356-8
ISBN-13: 978-0-13-440356-4

Dedications

For my husband Ted, who unselfishly continues to take on more than his share to support me throughout the process; and for my children, Laura, Carolyn, and Teddy, whose encouragement and love have been inspiring.

Mary Anne Poatsy

About the Authors

Mary Anne Poatsy, Author, Series Editor

Mary Anne is a senior faculty member at Montgomery County Community College, teaching various computer applications and concepts courses in face-to-face and online environments. She holds a B.A. in psychology and education from Mount Holyoke College and an M.B.A. in finance from Northwestern University's Kellogg Graduate School of Management.

Mary Anne has more than 12 years of educational experience. She is currently adjunct faculty at Gwynedd-Mercy College and Montgomery County Community College. She has also taught at Bucks County Community College and Muhlenberg College, as well as conducted personal training. Before teaching, she was Vice President at Shearson Lehman in the Municipal Bond Investment Banking Department.

Dr. Robert T. Grauer, Creator of the Exploring Series

Bob Grauer is an Associate Professor in the Department of Computer Information Systems at the University of Miami, where he is a multiple winner of the Outstanding Teaching Award in the School of Business, most recently in 2009. He has written numerous COBOL texts and is the vision behind the Exploring Office series, with more than three million books in print. His work has been translated into three foreign languages and is used in all aspects of higher education at both national and international levels. Bob Grauer has consulted for several major corporations including IBM and American Express. He received his Ph.D. in Operations Research in 1972 from the Polytechnic Institute of Brooklyn.

Contents

Acknowledgments

The Exploring team would like to acknowledge and thank all the reviewers who helped us throughout the years by providing us with their invaluable comments, suggestions, and constructive criticism.

Adriana Lumpkin
Midland College

Alan S. Abrahams
Virginia Tech

Alexandre C. Probst
Colorado Christian University

Ali Berrached
University of Houston–Downtown

Allen Alexander
Delaware Technical & Community College

Andrea Marchese
Maritime College, State University of New York

Andrew Blitz
Broward College; Edison State College

Angela Clark
University of South Alabama

Angel Norman
University of Tennessee, Knoxville

Ann Rovetto
Horry-Georgetown Technical College

Ann Rovetto
Horry-Georgetown Technical College

Astrid Todd
Guilford Technical Community College

Audrey Gillant
Maritime College, State University of New York

Barbara Stover
Marion Technical College

Barbara Tollinger
Sinclair Community College

Ben Brahim Taha
Auburn University

Beverly Amer
Northern Arizona University

Beverly Fite
Amarillo College

Biswadip Ghosh
Metropolitan State University of Denver

Bonita Volker
Tidewater Community College

Bonnie Homan
San Francisco State University

Brad West
Sinclair Community College

Brian Powell
West Virginia University

Brian Powell
West Virginia University

Carol Buser
Owens Community College

Carol Roberts
University of Maine

Carolyn Barren
Macomb Community College

Carolyn Barren
Macomb Community College

Carolyn Borne
Louisiana State University

Cathy Poyner
Truman State University

Charles Hodgson
Delgado Community College

Chen Zhang
Bryant University

Cheri Higgins
Illinois State University

Cheryl Brown
Delgado Community College

Cheryl Hinds
Norfolk State University

Cheryl Sypniewski
Macomb Community College

Chris Robinson
Northwest State Community College

Cindy Herbert
Metropolitan Community College–Longview

Craig J. Peterson
American InterContinental University

Dana Hooper
University of Alabama

Dana Johnson
North Dakota State University

Daniela Marghitu
Auburn University

David Noel
University of Central Oklahoma

David Pulis
Maritime College, State University of New York

David Thornton
Jacksonville State University

Dawn Medlin
Appalachian State University

Debby Keen
University of Kentucky

Debra Chapman
University of South Alabama

Debra Hoffman
Southeast Missouri State University

Derrick Huang
Florida Atlantic University

Diana Baran
Henry Ford Community College

Diane Cassidy
The University of North Carolina at Charlotte

Diane L. Smith
Henry Ford Community College

Diane Smith
Henry Ford Community College

Dick Hewer
Ferris State College

Doncho Petkov
Eastern Connecticut State University

Don Danner
San Francisco State University

Don Hoggan
Solano College

Donna Ehrhart
State University of New York at Brockport

Don Riggs
SUNY Schenectady County Community College

Elaine Crable
Xavier University

Elizabeth Duett
Delgado Community College

Erhan Uskup
Houston Community College–Northwest

Eric Martin
University of Tennessee

Erika Nadas
Wilbur Wright College

Floyd Winters
Manatee Community College

Frank Lucente
Westmoreland County Community College

G. Jan Wilms
Union University

Gail Cope
Sinclair Community College

Gary DeLorenzo
California University of Pennsylvania

Gary Garrison
Belmont University

Gary McFall
Purdue University

George Cassidy
Sussex County Community College

Gerald Braun
Xavier University

Gerald Burgess
Western New Mexico University

Gladys Swindler
Fort Hays State University

Hector Frausto
California State University
Los Angeles

Heith Hennel
Valencia Community College

Henry Rudzinski
Central Connecticut State University

Irene Joos
La Roche College

Iwona Rusin
Baker College; Davenport University

J. Roberto Guzman
San Diego Mesa College

Jacqueline D. Lawson
Henry Ford Community College

Jakie Brown Jr.
Stevenson University

James Brown
Central Washington University

James Powers
University of Southern Indiana

Jane Stam
Onondaga Community College

Janet Bringhurst
Utah State University

Jan Wilms
Union University

Jeanette Dix
Ivy Tech Community College

Jean Welsh
Lansing Community College

Jennifer Day
Sinclair Community College

Jill Canine
Ivy Tech Community College

Jill Young
Southeast Missouri State University

Jim Chaffee
The University of Iowa Tippie College of
Business

Joanne Lazirko
University of Wisconsin–Milwaukee

Jodi Milliner
Kansas State University

John Hollenbeck
Blue Ridge Community College

John Seydel
Arkansas State University

Judith A. Scheeren
Westmoreland County Community College

Judith Brown
The University of Memphis

Juliana Cypert
Tarrant County College

Kamaljeet Sanghera
George Mason University

Karen Priestly
Northern Virginia Community College

Karen Ravan
Spartanburg Community College

Karen Tracey
Central Connecticut State University

Kathleen Brenan
Ashland University

Ken Busbee
Houston Community College

Kent Foster
Winthrop University

Kevin Anderson
Solano Community College

Kim Wright
The University of Alabama

Kristen Hockman
University of Missouri–Columbia

Kristi Smith
Allegany College of Maryland

Laura Marcoulides
Fullerton College

Laura McManamon
University of Dayton

Laurence Boxer
Niagara University

Leanne Chun
Leeward Community College

Lee McClain
Western Washington University

Linda D. Collins
Mesa Community College

Linda Johnsonius
Murray State University

Linda Lau
Longwood University

Linda Theus
Jackson State Community College

Linda Williams
Marion Technical College

Lisa Miller
University of Central Oklahoma

Lister Horn
Pensacola Junior College

Lixin Tao
Pace University

Loraine Miller
Cayuga Community College

Lori Kielty
Central Florida Community College

Lorna Wells
Salt Lake Community College

Lorraine Sauchin
Duquesne University

Lucy Parakhovnik (Parker)
California State University,
Northridge

Lucy Parakhovnik
California State University, Northridge

Lynn Keane
University of South Carolina

Lynn Mancini
Delaware Technical Community College

Mackinzee Escamilla
South Plains College

Marcia Welch
Highline Community College

Margaret McManus
Northwest Florida State College

Margaret Warrick
Allan Hancock College

Marilyn Hibbert
Salt Lake Community College

Mark Choman
Luzerne County Community College

Maryann Clark
University of New Hampshire

Mary Beth Tarver
Northwestern State University

Mary Duncan
University of Missouri–St. Louis

Melissa Nemeth
Indiana University-Purdue University
Indianapolis

Melody Alexander
Ball State University

Michael Douglas
University of Arkansas at Little Rock

Michael Dunklebarger
Alamance Community College

Michael G. Skaff
College of the Sequoias

Michele Budnovitch
Pennsylvania College of Technology

Mike Jochen
East Stroudsburg University

Mike Michaelson
Palomar College

Mike Scroggins
Missouri State University

Mimi Spain
Southern Maine Community College

Muhammed Badamas
Morgan State University

NaLisa Brown
University of the Ozarks

Nancy Grant
Community College of Allegheny County–
South Campus

Nanette Lareau
University of Arkansas Community
College–Morrilton

Nikia Robinson
Indian River State University

Pam Brune
Chattanooga State Community College

Pam Uhlenkamp
Iowa Central Community College

Patrick Smith
Marshall Community and Technical College

Paul Addison
Ivy Tech Community College

Paula Ruby
Arkansas State University

Peggy Burrus
Red Rocks Community College

Peter Ross
SUNY Albany

Philip H. Nielson
Salt Lake Community College

Philip Valvalides
Guilford Technical Community College

Phil Nielson
Salt Lake Community College

Ralph Hooper
University of Alabama

Ranette Halverson
Midwestern State University

Richard Blamer
John Carroll University

Richard Cacace
Pensacola Junior College

Richard Hewer
Ferris State University

Richard Sellers
Hill College

Robert Banta
Macomb Community College

Robert Dušek
Northern Virginia Community College

Robert G. Phipps Jr.
West Virginia University

Robert Sindt
Johnson County Community College

Robert Warren
Delgado Community College

Rob Murray
Ivy Tech Community College

Rocky Belcher
Sinclair Community College

Roger Pick
University of Missouri at Kansas City

Ronnie Creel
Troy University

Rosalie Westerberg
Clover Park Technical College

Ruth Neal
Navarro College

Sandra Thomas
Troy University

Sheila Gionfriddo
Luzerne College

Sheila Gionfriddo
Luzerne County Community College

Sherrie Geitgey
Northwest State Community College

Sherry Lenhart
Terra Community College

Sophia Wilberscheid
Indian River State College

Sophie Lee
California State University,
Long Beach

Stacy Johnson
Iowa Central Community College

Stephanie Kramer
Northwest State Community College

Stephen Jourdan
Auburn University Montgomery

Stephen Z. Jourdan
Auburn University at Montgomery

Steven Schwarz
Raritan Valley Community College

Sue A. McCrory
Missouri State University

Sue McCrory
Missouri State University

Sumathy Chandrashekar
Salisbury University

Susan Fuschetto
Cerritos College

Susan Medlin
UNC Charlotte

Susan N. Dozier
Tidewater Community College

Suzanne M. Jeska
County College of Morris

Suzan Spitzberg
Oakton Community College

Sven Aelterman
Troy University

Sven Aelterman
Troy University

Sy Hirsch
Sacred Heart University

Sylvia Brown
Midland College

Tanya Patrick
Clackamas Community College

Terri Holly
Indian River State College

Terry Ray Rigsby
Hill College

Thomas Rienzo
Western Michigan University

Tina Johnson
Midwestern State University

Tommy Lu
Delaware Technical and Community
College

Tommy Lu
Delaware Technical Community College

Troy S. Cash
Northwest Arkansas Community College

Vickie Pickett
Midland College

Vicki Robertson
Southwest Tennessee Community

Wes Anthony
Houston Community College

Wilma Andrews
Virginia Commonwealth University

Weifeng Chen
California University of Pennsylvania

William Ayen
University of Colorado at Colorado Springs

Yvonne Galusha
University of Iowa

Special thanks to our content development and technical team:

Barbara Stover

Joyce Nielsen

Lori Damanti

Jean Insigna

Mike Gordon

Elizabeth Lockley

Preface

The Exploring Series

Exploring is Pearson's Office Application series that requires students to think "beyond the point and click." We focused this revision around the Learning Outcomes, Objectives, and Skills that make up this course as well as tailoring the learning experience around the way today's student actually uses his/her resources.

The goal of Exploring is, as it has always been, to go farther than teaching just the steps to accomplish a task—the series provides the theoretical foundation for students to understand when and why to apply a skill. As a result, students achieve a deeper understanding of each application and can apply this critical thinking beyond Office and the classroom.

The How & Why of This Revision

Outcomes matter. Whether it's getting a good grade in this course, learning how to use Excel so students can be successful in other courses, or learning a specific skill that will make learners successful in a future job, everyone has an outcome in mind. And outcomes matter. That is why we revised our chapter opener to focus on the outcomes students will achieve by working through each Exploring chapter. These are coupled with objectives and skills, providing a map students can follow to get everything they need from each chapter.

Critical Thinking and Collaboration are essential 21st century skills. Students want and need to be successful in their future careers—so we used motivating case studies to show relevance of these skills to future careers and incorporated Collaboration and Analysis Cases with Critical Thinking steps in this edition to set students up for success in the future.

Students today read, prepare, and study differently than students used to. Students use textbooks like a tool—they want to easily identify what they need to know and learn it efficiently. We have added key features such as Tasks Lists (in purple), Step Icons, Hands-On Exercise Videos, and tracked everything via page numbers that allow efficient navigation.

Students are exposed to technology. Exploring moves beyond the basics of the software at a faster pace, without sacrificing coverage of the fundamental skills that students need to know.

Students are diverse. Students can be any age, any gender, any race, with any level of ability or learning style. With this in mind, we broadened our definition of "student resources" to include physical Student Reference cards, Hands-On Exercise videos to provide a secondary lecture-like option of review, and MyITLab, the most powerful and most ADA-compliant online homework and assessment tool around with a direct 1:1 content match with the Exploring Series. Exploring will be accessible to all students, regardless of learning style.

Providing Students with a Map to Success to Move Beyond the Point and Click

All of these changes and additions will provide students an easy and efficient path to follow to be successful in this course, regardless of where they start at the beginning of this course. Our goal is to keep students engaged in both the hands-on and conceptual sides, helping achieve a higher level of understanding that will guarantee success in this course and in a future career.

In addition to the vision and experience of the series creator, Robert T. Grauer, we have assembled a tremendously talented team of Office Applications authors who have devoted themselves to teaching the ins and outs of Microsoft Word, Excel, Access, and PowerPoint. Led in this edition by series editor Mary Anne Poatsy, the whole team is dedicated to the Exploring mission of moving students **beyond the point and click**.

Key Features

The **How/Why Approach** helps students move beyond the point and click to a true understanding of how to apply Microsoft Office skills.

- **White Pages/Yellow Pages** clearly distinguish the theory (white pages) from the skills covered in the Hands-On Exercises (yellow pages) so students always know what they are supposed to be doing and why.

- **Case Study** presents a scenario for the chapter, creating a story that ties the Hands-On Exercises together.

- **Hands-On Exercise Videos** are tied to each Hands-On Exercise and walk students through the steps of the exercise while weaving in conceptual information related to the Case Study and the objectives as a whole.

The **Outcomes focus** allows students and instructors to know the higher level learning goals and how those are achieved through discreet objectives and skills.

- **Outcomes** presented at the beginning of each chapter identify the learning goals for students and instructors.

- **Enhanced Objective Mapping** enables students to follow a directed path through each chapter, from the objectives list at the chapter opener through the exercises in the end of chapter.
  - **Objectives List:** This provides a simple list of key objectives covered in the chapter. This includes page numbers so students can skip between objectives where they feel they need the most help.
  - **Step Icons:** These icons appear in the white pages and reference the step numbers in the Hands-On Exercises, providing a correlation between the two so students can easily find conceptual help when they are working hands-on and need a refresher.
  - **Quick Concepts Check:** A series of questions that appear briefly at the end of each white page section. These questions cover the most essential concepts in the white pages required for students to be successful in working the Hands-On Exercises. Page numbers are included for easy reference to help students locate the answers.
  - **Chapter Objectives Review:** Appears toward the end of the chapter and reviews all important concepts throughout the chapter. Newly designed in an easy-to-read bulleted format.

- **MOS Certification Guide** for instructors and students to direct anyone interested in prepping for the MOS exam to the specific locations to find all content required for the test.

End-of-Chapter Exercises offer instructors several options for assessment. Each chapter has approximately 11–12 exercises ranging from multiple choice questions to open-ended projects.

- **Multiple Choice, Key Terms Matching, Practice Exercises, Mid-Level Exercises, Beyond the Classroom Exercises, and Capstone Exercises** appear at the end of all chapters.
  - **Enhanced Mid-Level Exercises** include a **Creative Case** (for PowerPoint and Word), which allows students some flexibility and creativity, not being bound by a definitive solution, and an **Analysis Case** (for Excel and Access), which requires students to interpret the data they are using to answer an analytic question, as well as **Discover Steps**, which encourage students to use Help or to problem-solve to accomplish a task.

- **Application Capstone** exercises are included in the book to allow instructors to test students on the entire contents of a single application.

Resources

Instructor Resources

The Instructor's Resource Center, available at **www.pearsonhighered.com**, includes the following:

- **Instructor Manual** provides one-stop-shop for instructors, including an overview of all available resources, teaching tips, as well as student data and solution files for every exercise.

- **Solution Files with Scorecards** assist with grading the Hands-On Exercises and end-of-chapter exercises.

- **Prepared Exams** allow instructors to assess all skills covered in a chapter with a single project.

- **Rubrics** for Mid-Level Creative Cases and Beyond the Classroom Cases in Microsoft Word format enable instructors to customize the assignments for their classes.

- **PowerPoint Presentations** with notes for each chapter are included for out-of-class study or review.

- **Multiple Choice, Key Term Matching, and Quick Concepts Check Answer Keys**

- **Test Bank** provides objective-based questions for every chapter.

- **Scripted Lectures** offer an in-class lecture guide for instructors to mirror the Hands-On Exercises.

- **Syllabus Templates**

- **Outcomes, Objectives, and Skills List**

- **Assignment Sheet**

- **File Guide**

Student Resources

Student Data Files

Access student data files needed to complete the exercises in this textbook at **www.pearson highered. com/exploring**.

Available in MyITLab

- **Hands-On Exercise Videos** allow students to review and study the concepts taught in the Hands-On Exercises.
- **Audio PowerPoints** provide a lecture review of the chapter content and include narration.
- **Multiple Choice Quizzes** enable students to test concepts by answering auto-graded questions.
- **Topic-Based Simulations** allow students to practice in the simulated Windows 10 environment using hi-fidelity HTML5 simulations.
- **eText** available in some MyITLab courses.

Working with an Operating System

LEARNING OUTCOMES:
- You will manage the Windows 10 environment through the desktop and other components.
- You will organize files and folders using Windows 10 features and tools.

OBJECTIVES & SKILLS: After you read this chapter, you will be able to:

CASE STUDY | Cedar Grove Elementary School

Your good friend recently graduated with a degree in elementary education and now is excited to begin her first job as a fifth-grade teacher at Cedar Grove Elementary School. The school has a computer lab for all students as well as a computer system in each classroom. The school acquired the computers through a state technology grant so they are new models running Windows 10. Your friend's lesson plans must include a unit on operating system basics and an introduction to application software. Because you have a degree in computer information systems, she has called on you for assistance with the lesson plans.

You cannot assume that all students are exposed to computers at home, especially to those configured with Windows 10. Your material will need to include very basic instruction on Windows 10, along with a general overview of file management. Your friend must complete her lesson plans right away, so you are on a short timeline but are excited about helping students learn!

Getting Started with Microsoft®
Windows® 10

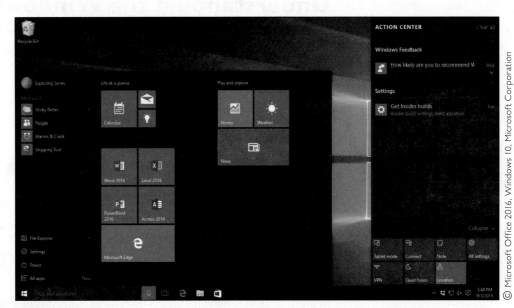

FIGURE 1.1 The Windows 10 Start Menu

CASE STUDY | Cedar Grove Elementary School

Starting Files	Files to Submit
Blank Word Document	**win01h3Windows10_LastFirst**

Windows 10 Fundamentals

There are two types of software on your computer: application software and system software. Application software are programs you use for email, gaming, social networking, and digital photo management. Application software also includes productivity software such as word processing, spreadsheet, and presentation applications. As essential as these application programs may be to you for entertainment or for accomplishing a specific task, system software is the essential software that the computer needs. Without system software, your computer could not function. System software includes the operating system and utility programs, and helps to run application software, manage your files, and manage system resources and other computer activities.

In this section, you will learn how to work with the features of the Windows 10 operating system. In particular, you will learn how to set up a Microsoft account, if you do not have one established already, and start and shut down Windows. You will also learn how to configure the Start menu and taskbar to manage programs and apps.

Understanding the Windows 10 Interface

Windows 10 is the latest version of Microsoft's operating system and is available for desktops, laptops, cell phones, and tablet computers. Windows 10 has made changes that facilitate computer use, both on touch and non-touch devices. Because you are likely to encounter Windows 10 on computers and mobile devices at school, work, and home, it is well worth your time to explore and learn how to use it, as well as its computer management and security features.

Sign In to a Microsoft Account

When you start your computer, Windows 10 opens to the Lock screen that displays an image (which you can personalize with your own image) and the date and time. Clicking on the Lock screen brings you to the sign in page where you log in using your Microsoft account username (email address) and password. To use any Microsoft services such as Outlook.com, Xbox Live®, OneDrive®, and Office Online, you need to create a free Microsoft account.

If you already have a OneDrive, Xbox Live, or Outlook.com account, use that account to sign in. If you do not have a Microsoft account, you will need to create one to use Windows 10. A Microsoft account gives you a consistent experience across any device you sign into with your Microsoft account. In addition, you get access to Office Online and OneDrive (with free cloud storage), and all your information syncs across all your devices.

To sign up for a Microsoft account, complete the following steps:

1. Open any Web browser, type signup.live.com as the URL, and then click Sign up now.
2. Fill out the form by typing your first and last name.

   Your user name will be an email address. You can use an existing email address, or you can get a new email address by clicking *Or get a new email address*.
3. Create a password that has at least 8 characters.

   To create a strong password, use a combination of upper and lowercase letters, at least one number and one other character (such as an asterisk or exclamation point).
4. Fill out the rest of the form, and then click Create account.

Access Sleep and Power Settings

To save battery life on your laptop, tablet, or smartphone, or for more energy efficiency, Windows will go to *sleep* after a pre-determined period of inactivity. Sleep is a power-saving state that puts your work and settings in memory and draws a small amount of power that allows your computer to resume full-power operation quickly.

To manage the Sleep settings, complete the following steps:

1. Click the Start icon or press the Windows key to open the Start menu.
2. Click Settings on the Start menu, click System, and then click Power & sleep.
3. Select the desired level of inactivity from any of the following options:
   - Screen: to determine when the Screen turns off on battery power or when plugged in
   - Sleep: to determine when the PC goes to sleep on battery power or when plugged in

Eventually, you will want to shut down Windows and turn off your computer. To do so, from the Start menu, click Power. Selecting Restart will turn off and immediately restart Windows. This is a "warm boot." To power down completely, click Power and then select Shut down.

Explore the Windows 10 Start Menu

After signing in, you should see the same screen configuration no matter what Windows 10 device you are using, because your Microsoft account stores your preferences and settings for your Start menu on the Internet. For instance, your laptop computer, your home computer, and even your Windows smartphone should look the same.

Initially, your computer displays the primary working area: the *desktop*. If you were used to working on a system running Windows 8, you will notice that there is not a Start screen and a desktop. Instead, the desktop is the primary working area of Windows 10, and the Windows 10 *Start menu* provides the main access to all programs and features on your computer.

There are three different ways to accomplish tasks in Windows 10:

- Use a mouse
- Touch v the screen (on touch-enabled devices)
- Use keystrokes

The method you use depends on the type of device you are using and, largely, on your personal preferences. In this text, we will focus mainly on mouse and keystroke commands. If you are using a touch-screen device, you should refer to the new touch gestures shown in Figure 1.2. For instance, when an instruction in this text says to click a screen element, you would tap the screen element with your finger on a touch-screen device.

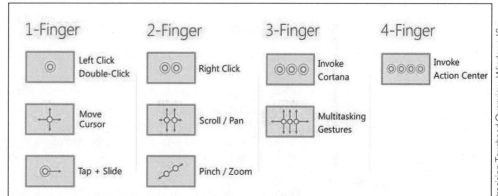

FIGURE 1.2 Touch Gestures in Windows 10

Open the Start menu by clicking the Start icon in the bottom left corner of the desktop or by pressing the Windows key on the keyboard. The Start menu, as shown in Figure 1.3, has two areas. The right side has the same look as the metro (or modern) view first introduced in Windows 8 with block icons, called *tiles*. Tiles represent installed programs and Windows apps (such as Weather, Skype, and Money). Tiles can also represent files, folders, or other items related to your computer. If there are more tiles on the Start menu than displayed, use the scroll bar on the right. You can launch Windows 10 apps and programs by clicking or tapping a tile on the Start menu.

TIP: STICKY NOTE APP

Sticky Notes is a useful Windows accessory application. Use Sticky Notes as you would a paper sticky note, recording to-do lists, phone numbers, or anything else. Your notes display on the desktop. Sticky Notes is found in the Windows Accessories folder in All apps. Click New Note to add another note, click Delete Note to delete a note, and right-click a note to change the color.

Most used program list

Program tiles & Tile Groups

File Explorer, Settings, Power, All apps

FIGURE 1.3 Windows 10 Start Menu

The left side of the Start menu provides access to File Explorer, Settings, and Power. These features are discussed later in this chapter. There is also a separate *Most used* section that contains a list of apps and programs you use every day. However, you can remove a program from the Most used list by right-clicking the icon and selecting *Don't show in this list*. Click *All apps* at the bottom of the left pane, and the left pane changes to display a list of all installed apps and programs on your computer, in alphabetical order.

Configure the Start Menu

STEP 1 ⟫ You may want to customize the Start menu so you can use it most efficiently. It is easy to add and remove, resize, and move application tiles on the Start menu, as well as to group tiles, and name the groups. You can also display tiles to access folders or other areas of the computer that you use frequently. You *pin*, or add, a tile to the Start menu to make it easier to access the application.

To pin an application to the Start menu, complete the following steps:

1. Display the Start menu by clicking Start on the taskbar or by pressing the Windows key on your keyboard.
2. Click All apps and find the application that you want to pin to the Start menu.
3. Right-click the app name and select Pin to Start. (You may also choose Pin to taskbar. The taskbar is discussed later in this chapter.) A tile for the app displays on the Start menu. The new tile is added to the very end of your app tiles, so you may have to scroll down to find the tile you added.

Once on the Start menu, the size of a tile can be modified.

To resize a tile on the Start menu, complete the following steps:

1. Right-click the tile and point to Resize.
2. Select from the list of available sizes: Small, Medium, Wide, or Large.

You may also have some tiles that you do not want on the Start menu. These might be programs or applications that appear on the Start menu by default, or tiles you added but now want to remove. Removing (or unpinning) an application is just as easy as adding one.

To unpin an application from the Start menu, complete the following steps:

1. Right-click the tile you want to remove from the Start menu.
2. Click Unpin from Start to remove the tile from the Start menu.

Tiles on the Start menu are organized in groups separated by a small amount of dividing space, as shown in Figure 1.3. You can easily move tiles from one group to another by clicking a tile and dragging it into another group. You can reorder groups by clicking the group name and dragging the group to its new location. You can also give any group of tiles a meaningful name.

To create a new group of tiles, complete the following steps:

1. Click and drag the first tile for the new group to the space above or below an existing tile group. An empty bar displays, indicating where the new group will be located.
2. Release the mouse button, and the tile will now be in its own new group.

To assign a new name to a group of tiles, complete the following steps:

1. Point near the top of the tile or group of tiles you want to name.
2. Click in the box that displays.
3. Type a new group name. Note, if a name exists, you can delete the existing name and then type a new name.

Explore the Taskbar

At the bottom of the Windows desktop is the *taskbar*. The taskbar is the horizontal bar that displays open application icons, the *Notification area*, the *search box*, and any pinned apps or programs. The Notification area, at the far right of the taskbar, includes the clock and a group of icons that relate to a status of a setting or program. The search box, located on the left side of the taskbar, can be used to search your computer for programs, folders and files saved on your computer, as well as to get results from the Web. The Search bar is also home to Cortana, the personal digital assistant. Cortana is discussed later in this chapter.

Every open program has a corresponding icon on the taskbar. You can move from one program to another by clicking the program's icon on the taskbar. Figure 1.4 shows two windows open on the desktop, with corresponding taskbar program icons. A blue line displays under the open program icons. Although several windows can be open at one time, only one is active. The active program icon is shaded with a lighter blue background. When you right-click a program icon, you open the *Jump List* (see Figure 1.4). A Jump List is a list of program-specific shortcuts to recently opened files, the program name, an option to pin or unpin an item, and a Close windows option.

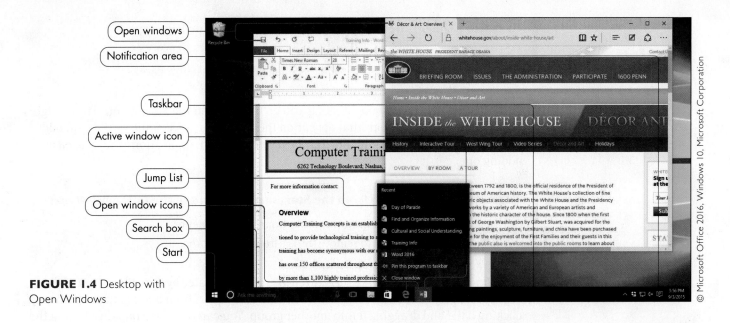

Open windows
Notification area
Taskbar
Active window icon
Jump List
Open window icons
Search box
Start

FIGURE 1.4 Desktop with Open Windows

TIP: HIDE THE TASKBAR

Although it is very helpful, the taskbar can occupy space on your work area that you may need. To temporarily hide the taskbar, right-click an empty area of the taskbar. Click Properties. In the Taskbar and Start Menu Properties dialog box, click the check box to select *Auto-hide the taskbar*, and then click OK. The taskbar immediately disappears. When you move the pointer to the previous location of the taskbar, it will appear, but only until you move the pointer away. To return the taskbar to view, reverse the process described above, clicking the check box to deselect *Auto-hide the taskbar*.

Similar to pinning an app or program to the Start menu, you can place, or pin, icons of frequently used programs or websites on the taskbar for faster access. When you pin a program or website to the taskbar, its associated icon becomes a permanent part of the taskbar. You can then open the program or website by clicking its icon.

To pin to the taskbar a program that is not already open, complete the following steps:

1. Locate the program in All apps.
2. Right-click the program name.
3. Click Pin to taskbar.

To pin to the taskbar a program that is already open, complete the following steps:

1. Right-click the program icon on the taskbar.
2. Click Pin this program to taskbar.

You will find the Notification area (refer to Figure 1.4) on the right side of the taskbar. This area contains system icons, including Clock, Volume, OneDrive, and Action Center. The Notification area and what icons display in the Notification area are discussed later in this chapter.

Identify Desktop Components

The desktop in Windows 10 looks very much like the desktop in previous versions of Windows. On the desktop, *icons* represent links to programs, files, folders, or other items related to your computer (see Figure 1.5). Although the Start menu is meant to provide quick access to programs, files and folders you use most often, you can easily add and remove icons so that the desktop includes items that are important to you or that you access often.

The Recycle Bin icon displays by default on the Windows 10 desktop. The **Recycle Bin** is temporary storage for deleted files from the computer's hard drive or OneDrive. Files in the Recycle Bin are not permanently erased from the system until you right-click the Recycle Bin icon and select Empty Recycle Bin. Therefore, if you delete a file by mistake, it can be restored. The exception is if the file was from an external storage device such as a flash drive. When you delete files from an external storage device, they are permanently deleted.

Recycle Bin

Folder

Program shortcut

FIGURE 1.5 Desktop Components

Some icons that have a small arrow in the bottom-left corner are *shortcuts* that provide a link to programs. All other icons on the desktop are added when you save a file to the desktop. If you save files to the desktop, you should organize them in desktop folders so you can easily find related files.

To add a program or folder shortcut icon to the desktop, complete the following steps:

1. Right-click an empty area of the desktop, point to New, and then click Shortcut.
2. Click Browse and navigate to the folder that contains the program for which you wish to create a shortcut.
3. Click the program file and click OK.
4. Click Next. Type a name for the shortcut in the box
5. Click Finish to place the shortcut icon on your desktop.

You can also add a folder directly to the desktop by right-clicking an empty area of the desktop, pointing to New, and then selecting Folder. Or, if there is an existing folder you want to add to the desktop, open File Explorer, right-click the folder, choose Send to, and then select Desktop (create shortcut) from the menu.

To delete or rename icons on the desktop, complete one of the following steps:

- Right-click the icon you want to delete, and click Delete. Deleting a program shortcut icon does not remove or uninstall the program. You just remove the desktop shortcut to the program.
- Right-click the icon you want to rename, and click Rename. Type the new name and press Enter.

TIP: AUTO ARRANGE ICONS

A desktop can easily become cluttered and disorganized. To avoid clutter, make sure that you maintain only desktop icons that are accessed often or that are important to keep handy. To neatly organize the desktop, you can auto arrange the icons. Right-click an empty area of the desktop, point to View, and select *Auto arrange icons* (unless *Auto arrange icons* already has a checkmark). Icons are displayed in straight columns and cannot be moved out of line. You can also sort the icons on the desktop by Name, Size, Item type, or Date modified. Doing so can help you find an item on a cluttered desktop. To sort desktop icons, right-click an empty area of the desktop, point to Sort by, and select the sort method.

Customize the Desktop

For a little variety, you can customize the desktop with a different background color or theme. You can even include a slide show of favorite photos to display when your computer is idle. Customizing the desktop can be fun and creative. Windows 10 provides a wide selection of background and color choices.

The Personalization category in Settings gives you options to change the desktop background, lock screen image, or to select a different theme.

Managing and Using the Desktop and Components

The main purpose of the Start menu is to provide access to programs and apps. To launch an app or program from the Start menu, click the app tile. **Windows apps**, such as Weather, Sports, or Money, are programs that are displayed full screen without borders or many controls. This simpler design provides a viewing advantage on devices with smaller screens such as smartphones and tablets. Controls and settings are contained on app bars, such as the Address bar, which appear at the top or bottom of the opened app. Installed programs such as Microsoft Word or Google Chrome are applications that are more complex. They generally have multiple features and can perform multiple tasks.

TIP: THE SNIPPING TOOL

The Snipping Tool is a Windows accessory application that enables you to capture, or **snip**, a screen display so that you can save, annotate, or share it. You can capture screen elements in a rectangular, free-form, window, or full-screen snip. You can also draw on or annotate the screen captures, save them, or send them to others. New to Windows 10 is a delay feature in the Snipping Tool that pauses the program from capturing a screenshot for up to 5 minutes. You cannot use the Snipping Tool, however, to capture Windows elements such as the Start menu or dialog boxes. For those features, you will need to use the Print Screen key.

Using the taskbar, you can move among open windows with ease, but Windows provides additional methods to switch easily between open programs and files. Windows makes it easy to move, resize, and close windows, as well as to arrange windows automatically, even snapping them quickly to the desktop borders.

Use Task View

STEP 2 ⟩⟩ It is quite possible that you will have more than one application or program window open at any time, and may need to quickly switch between the various open windows or want to see two or more open windows at the same time. ***Task View*** allows you to view all the tasks you are working on in one glance (see Figure 1.6). For example, you might have Microsoft Word, PowerPoint, and Edge all open because you are creating a presentation from your latest research paper and are doing some extra Internet research. To see all three windows at once, click the Task View icon next to the search box in the taskbar, and thumbnail previews of all open applications display. Click on any of the thumbnails to switch to that application.

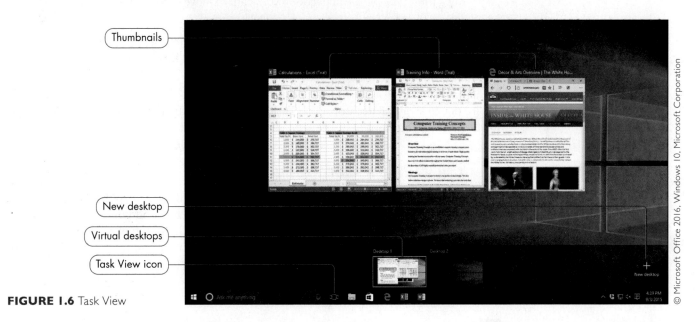

FIGURE 1.6 Task View

TIP: ALT+TAB

You can use the keyboard to cycle through all open windows. Press and hold Alt on the keyboard and repeatedly press Tab. Release Alt when the window that you want to display is selected.

Create a Virtual Desktop

Task View also enables you to create ***virtual desktops*** (refer to Figure 1.6). A virtual desktop is a way to organize and access groups of windows for different purposes. For example, when you do your schoolwork, you might have your school's learning management system (such as Blackboard or Desire to Learn), your school's email account, and MyITLab open. When you are not working on schoolwork, you might have several social media accounts open, perhaps a video game, and maybe Netflix or YouTube running. Using Task View, you can group these applications into virtual desktops, so that you can quickly switch between your "school" desktop and your "entertainment" desktop.

To create a new virtual desktop and move applications between desktops, complete the following steps:

1. Click Task View on the taskbar, and click New desktop in the lower right corner of your screen.

   You will then see a thumbnail preview of the new desktop (Desktop 2) alongside the current desktop (in this case, Desktop 1). Once the new desktop is created, you will need to populate it with applications by moving applications from one desktop to another.

2. Click Desktop 1, and then click Task View.
3. Drag a thumbnail of the application you want to move from Desktop 1 to Desktop 2.
4. Repeat as needed to create a new virtual desktop.
5. Alternatively, right-click a thumbnail preview of any open application in Desktop 1, point to Move to, and either select an existing virtual desktop or create a new desktop.

To delete a virtual desktop, click Task View, point to the top right corner of the desktop thumbnail you want to delete, and click the Close button.

Identify Window Components

When you launch a folder, file, or application, the results are displayed in a window. All windows share common elements, including a title bar and controls, as shown in Figure 1.7. Although each window's contents vary, those common elements make it easy for you to manage windows so that you make the best use of your time and computer resources.

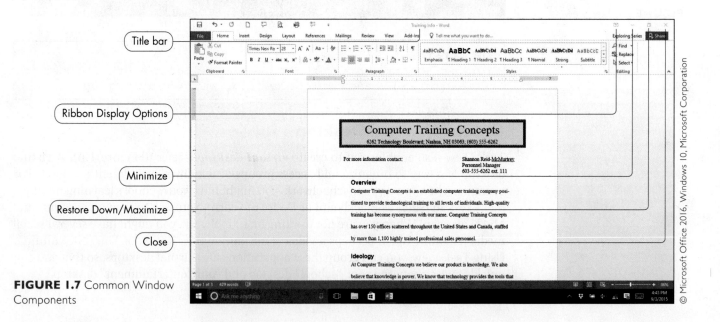

FIGURE 1.7 Common Window Components

The *title bar* is the long bar at the top of each window. The title bar always displays the name of the folder, file, or program displayed in the open window. Controls are found on the right side of the title bar. These controls enable you to manage the Ribbon display as well as to minimize, maximize (or restore down), or close any open window.

The Ribbon Display Options control enables you to hide the Ribbon, show only the Ribbon tabs, or to show the Ribbon tabs and commands all the time.

The Minimize control, represented by a horizontal line, when clicked hides a window from view, but does not close it. You can click on the taskbar icon to view the window again.

The next control shares two functions, depending on the current size of the window. When a window is full size, Restore Down, represented by two overlapping boxes, displays. When a window is open, but less than full size, Maximize, represented by a small box, displays. Clicking Restore Down returns a window to the size it was before the window was maximized; clicking Maximize brings a window to full size. You can also maximize or restore down a window by double-clicking the title bar of the open window.

The Close control, represented by an X, when clicked closes a window. When you close a window, you remove the file or program from the computer's random access memory (RAM). RAM is temporary (or volatile) storage, meaning files stored in RAM are not permanently saved. To save a file so you can access it later, the file must be saved to a permanent storage device such as the computer's hard drive or a flash drive, or to OneDrive or other Web-based storage. If you have not saved a file, or any changes that you have made to a saved file that you are closing, Windows 10 will prompt you to save it.

Snap, Move, and Resize Windows

STEP 3 ▶▶ Multitasking involves working with multiple open windows at the same time, and this often requires moving or resizing windows so you can see each window. If multiple windows are open, you will need to know how to switch between windows and how to rearrange them. Windows 7 introduced "snapping" windows—displaying two windows side by side by snapping them to the left and right sides of the screen.

To snap windows side by side, complete the following steps:

1. Drag the title bar of a window to the left or right side of the screen until an outline of the expanded window appears.
2. Release the mouse button to expand the window.
3. Repeat steps 1 and 2 with another window, dragging to the opposite side of the display.

Windows 10 goes a bit further with Snap Assist, giving you more snapping options. For example, once you snap one window to either side of the display, thumbnails of all other open windows display (Figure 1.8) giving you the option of easily selecting which window(s) to snap alongside it.

To use Snap Assist, complete the following steps:

1. Snap one window to either side of the screen.

   Thumbnails of all other open windows display on the open portion of the screen.
2. Click the thumbnail you want to snap, or click in a blank area if you do not want to snap any of the choices.

   The selected window will snap into place, filling the open screen area.
3. Press the Windows key plus an arrow key once windows are snapped to either side of the screen to snap windows into corners. You can snap two, three, or four windows using this technique. Alternatively, you can drag a window to the corner of the screen.

Instead of snapping, there might be occasions when you want to work with multiple files that are more freely positioned, without snapping them to the edges. In these instances, you can restore down a window, modify the size, and drag the smaller window to any location on the screen.

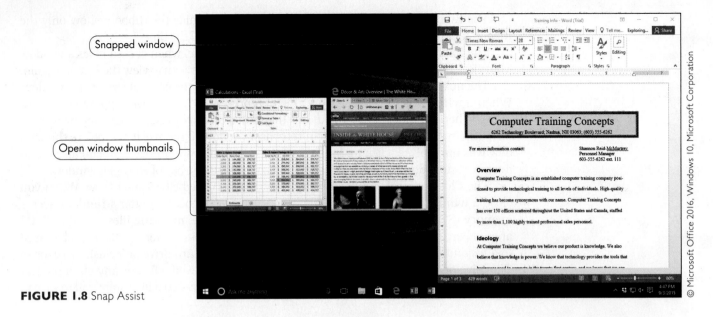

Snapped window

Open window thumbnails

FIGURE 1.8 Snap Assist

To move or resize a window, you must first click Restore Down and then complete one of the following steps:

- Click and drag the title bar to move a window.
- Point to the border of a window you want to resize, until the pointer becomes a double-headed arrow. Then, click and drag the edge of a window to make the window larger or smaller. If the pointer is on a corner of the window, forming a diagonal double-headed arrow, the height and width of the window will resize at the same time.

You might prefer to let Windows arrange your windows automatically in a cascading fashion, vertically stacked, or next to each other. In that case, right-click an empty part of the taskbar. Then, click Cascade windows, Show windows stacked, or Show windows side by side.

Using Windows 10 Search Features

The new design of Windows 10 makes it easy to organize and find the most used programs, files and folders on either the Start menu, taskbar, or desktop. However, there will always be situations that require you to find a feature or file that you do not often use, and are not certain of its location, or you may need to find information on the Web. In those cases, you will need to use Windows 10 search features.

Use the Search Box

 To the right of the Start button is the search box. You can use this search feature to search the Web and to search your "stuff" in Windows. When you begin typing into the search box, suggested results begin to display with a list of applications, folders, and documents, as well as Web resources that relate to the search terms you have entered (see Figure 1.9).

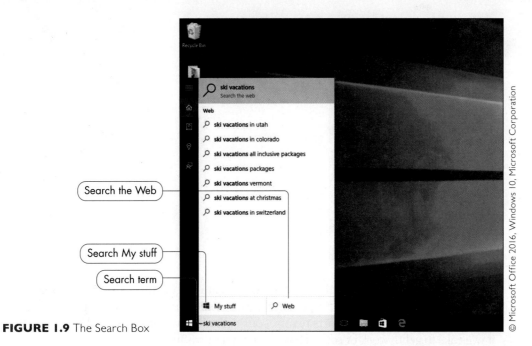

Search the Web

Search My stuff

Search term

FIGURE 1.9 The Search Box

No longer do you have to go to a separate location on your computer, or use a different app, to get help. Type into the search box whatever question you have, and whether the answer is found in a file, an app, on the Web, or somewhere else, a list of possible results will display. Just click on the answer that best meets your needs.

Use Cortana

If you have logged into Windows with your Microsoft account, you can use **Cortana**, Microsoft's personal assistant. Cortana is integrated into the search box and can assist you with reminders, calendar tasks, and can even tell jokes. You must initiate Cortana first, by giving her your name, and allowing her access to your information. Then, if your PC is equipped with a microphone, you begin talking to Cortana by saying, "Hey, Cortana." If no microphone is available, you can type all your questions.

Get Help

STEP 5 ›› Cortana and the search box are your primary resources for help and support for Windows and other Microsoft related questions. Just type into the search box, or ask Cortana, and you will get information about using Windows and quick access to various Windows settings. Search results may also display how-to information and videos from Microsoft. You can even type the name of an app to open it right away. Finally, Cortana can help you with routine tasks such as turning on Airplane mode, just ask her!

Manage the Cortana Notebook and Settings

The more you use Cortana, the more she adapts to your personal needs and routines. When you initiate Cortana, you agree to let her collect and use some personal information that she has obtained from data on your PC (such as your location, contacts, info from email, browser history, search history, and .calendar details). Once you set up Cortana, your data and information is managed in the Notebook. You can modify what Cortana remembers (or turn Cortana off altogether) in the Notebook.

> **To view or modify what is in the Notebook, complete the following steps:**
>
> 1. Click the search box, and then click Notebook from the menu on the left.
>
>   You will see categories that have been added by default, such as Eat & Drink, Events, Finance, and Getting around.
>
> 2. Click any category to change a setting or add more information to the Notebook.
>
>   There are many categories and subcategories from which to choose (see Figure 1.10).

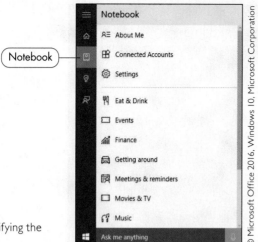

FIGURE 1.10 Modifying the Cortana Notebook

Once you have modified the settings, and you launch Cortana, the Home page shows a daily glance that reflects your personal settings such as the weather in your location, the scores of your favorite sports teams, your calendar events, and even how much time it will take to get to work or school based on current traffic.

You can modify other items such as Reminders, Places, and Music directly from the Cortana menu (see Figure 1.11).

FIGURE 1.11 Cortana Notebook Menu Item

Quick Concepts

1. Describe the features on the Start menu, and explain the various ways in which the Start menu can be customized. *pp. 5–7*

2. Explain what a virtual desktop is, and give an example of how you would use virtual desktops for school, work, or entertainment. *p. 11*

3. Review some of the features Cortana offers, and give some specific examples of modifications you would make in the Cortana Notebook to reflect your personal needs. *p. 15*

4. What features can you use to get help and support on Windows 10? *p. 15*

Hands-On Exercise

Watch the Video for This Hands-On Exercise!

MyITLab®
Topic-Based Training

Skills covered: Pin an App to Start Menu • Create Start Menu Group • Rename Start Menu Group • Move Tile • Resize Tile • Pin App to the Taskbar • Create Virtual Desktop • Minimize, Close, Restore Down, Maximize • Snap Windows • Search Using Cortana • Manage Cortana Settings • Get Help

1 Windows 10 Fundamentals

Tomorrow, you will meet with the Cedar Grove class to present an introduction to Windows 10. You plan to lead the students through a few basics of working with the operating system, including managing the Start menu and navigating among different open windows. Above all, you want to keep it simple so that you encourage class enthusiasm.

STEP 1 ⟩⟩ CONFIGURE THE START MENU AND EXPLORE THE TASKBAR

You want to emphasize the importance of the Start menu as the location starting point for all Windows 10 apps and programs. Students will practice launching, managing, and closing Windows 10 apps and programs. Students will modify the Start menu by creating a new group and moving a tile into the group. Lastly, students will add program icons to the taskbar. Refer to Figure 1.12 as you complete Step 1.

FIGURE 1.12 Customizing the Start Menu and Taskbar

a. Click **Start** on the taskbar (or alternatively, press the Windows key on the keyboard).

The Start menu displays.

b. Click **Word 2016** on the Start menu, and click **Blank document**.

> **TROUBLESHOOTING:** Microsoft Word may be displayed as a tile, or in the Most used group. If Microsoft Word does not display in the Start menu, click All apps, and scroll to locate the program. It might be in the Microsoft Office folder.

c. Click **File**, select **Save As**, and then click **Browse.** Navigate to the location of your homework files. Click in the **File name** box and type **win01h1Windows10_LastFirst**, replacing LastFirst with your own last name and first name in the File name box. Click **Save** to save the document.

When you save files, use your last and first names. For example, as the Windows 10 author, I would name my document "win01h1Windows10_PoatsyMaryAnne."

You will capture screenshots of your progress in this exercise and paste them into this document to submit to your instructor.

d. Click the **Start menu**, click **All apps**, and then scroll down to locate the Windows Accessories folder. Click the **down arrow** to display the contents of the Windows Accessories folder, and then locate Snipping Tool. Right-click **Snipping Tool**, and select **Pin to Start**.

The Snipping Tool tile displays on the Start menu. You will use the Snipping Tool in a later exercise.

> **TROUBLESHOOTING:** Depending on the configuration of tiles on your Start menu, you may need to scroll to see the Snipping Tool tile. Or, the Snipping Tool tile may already be pinned.

e. Point in the blank space just above the Snipping Tool tile and click to open a name box. Type **Useful Windows Apps**, and press **Enter**.

You have created a new group on the Start menu that includes the Snipping Tool.

f. Click **All apps**, open the Windows Accessories folder, right-click **Sticky Notes** and select **Pin to Start**.

The Sticky Notes tile is added to the Start menu.

g. Drag the Sticky Notes tile into the Useful Windows Apps group you just created.

The new group has two tiles.

> **TROUBLESHOOTING:** Depending on the number and the configuration of tiles on your Start menu, you may need to scroll to see the Sticky Notes tile.

h. Drag the **title bar** of the Useful Windows Apps group so that the new group is at the top left corner of the Start menu tiles section.

You have repositioned the Useful Windows Apps group to a place that is more easily accessible on the Start menu.

i. Right-click the **Snipping Tool tile**, point to **Resize**, and then click **Small**.

You have resized the Snipping Tool tile so that it is smaller.

j. Right-click the **Snipping Tool tile** again, point to **Resize**, and then click **Medium**.

You realize that you like the larger tile, so you resized it back to the larger size.

k. Keep the Start menu open, press **Print Screen (PrtSc)** on your keyboard, click **Word** on the taskbar, and then press **Ctrl+V** on your keyboard. Click **Save** on the Quick Access Toolbar in the upper left corner of the Word window.

You have captured an image of your screen and pasted it into a Word document.

> **TROUBLESHOOTING:** If you have minimized the Word window, you will need to click the thumbnail to first maximize the Word window before pasting the Print Screen image.

l. Right-click **Word** on the taskbar, and click **Pin this program to taskbar**.

Right-clicking an icon on the taskbar opens the Jump List and the option to pin the program to the taskbar.

m. Display the Word Jump List again, press **Print Screen (PrtSc)**, click the **Word window**, press **Enter** twice, and then press **Ctrl+V**.

n. Save the document.

STEP 2 **》** **USE TASK VIEW AND CREATE A VIRTUAL DESKTOP**

Not only do you want students to understand the basics of managing apps and windows, but also you know they will enjoy customizing the Start menu. Refer to Figure 1.13 as you complete Step 2.

FIGURE 1.13 Task View and Virtual Desktops

a. Click **Minimize** (the horizontal line button) in the top right corner of the Word window. Click **Task View** on the taskbar.

A large thumbnail of the Word window displays.

b. Click the **Word thumbnail** to activate the Word window.

c. Open the **Start menu**, and click **Microsoft Edge** in the Most used section of the Start menu, type **usa.gov** in the Address bar, and then press **Enter**.

You have opened the Microsoft Edge browser application and navigated to usa.gov, the United States government's official Web portal.

> **TROUBLESHOOTING:** Microsoft Edge may not be in the Most used section of the Start menu. It may be on the Start menu or click All apps, and then scroll to locate Microsoft Edge. Alternatively, type Microsoft Edge in Cortana.

d. Click **Start** to return to the Start menu.

e. Click the **Calendar tile** on the Start menu.

You have now launched the Calendar app. Most likely, the calendar will not have any data in it, unless you have previously entered items in the Calendar app.

> **TROUBLESHOOTING:** If the Calendar app is not on the Start menu, click another Windows 10 app such as Sports, Money, or Weather.

f. Click **Task View**.

The Calendar, Microsoft Edge, and Word thumbnails display on the desktop.

g. Click **New desktop** on the bottom right corner of the desktop.

Two desktop thumbnails display at the bottom of the desktop. Desktop 1 thumbnail displays the three open apps. The Desktop 2 thumbnail is blank.

h. Point to the **Desktop 1 thumbnail** to display thumbnails of the three open apps on Desktop 1. Drag the Calendar thumbnail to Desktop 2.

i. Press **PrtSc**, click the **Word thumbnail**, press **Enter** twice, and then press **Ctrl+V**. Save the document.

STEP 3 ▶▶ SNAP, MOVE, AND RESIZE WINDOWS

Because there will be occasions when several windows are open simultaneously on the desktop, students should know how to arrange them. You will show them various ways that Windows 10 can help arrange open windows. Refer to Figure 1.14 as you complete Step 3.

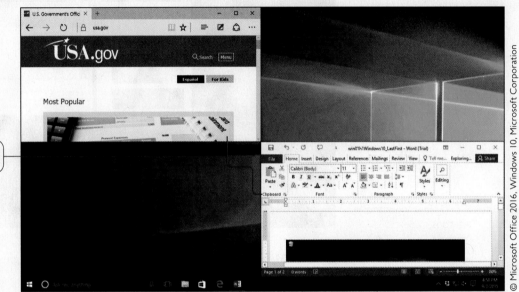

Steps c and d: Windows snapped to corners

FIGURE 1.14 Arrange Windows Using Snap

a. Click and hold the left mouse button on the **title bar of the Word window**. Drag the window to the far right of the screen until you see an outline of the window display. Release the mouse button.

The Word window snaps to the right side of the display, and a thumbnail of the Microsoft Edge window is in the left side of the display.

b. Click the **Microsoft Edge thumbnail**.

The Microsoft Edge window automatically snaps to the left side of the display.

c. Press and hold the **Windows key**, and then press ⬆ to snap the Microsoft Edge window to the top left corner.

d. Click the **Word window**, press and hold the **Windows key**, and then press ⬇.

The Word window snaps to the bottom right corner.

e. Press **PrtSc**, click **Maximize** on the Word window, press **Enter** twice, and then press **Ctrl+V**. Right-click **Microsoft Edge** on the taskbar, click **Close window**.

f. Save and close the Word file.

Since Cortana is a cool feature of Windows 10, you want students to learn how to use it. You will show the students how to use Cortana to search for a file, schedule a reminder, and even how to tell a joke. Refer to Figure 1.15 as you complete Step 4.

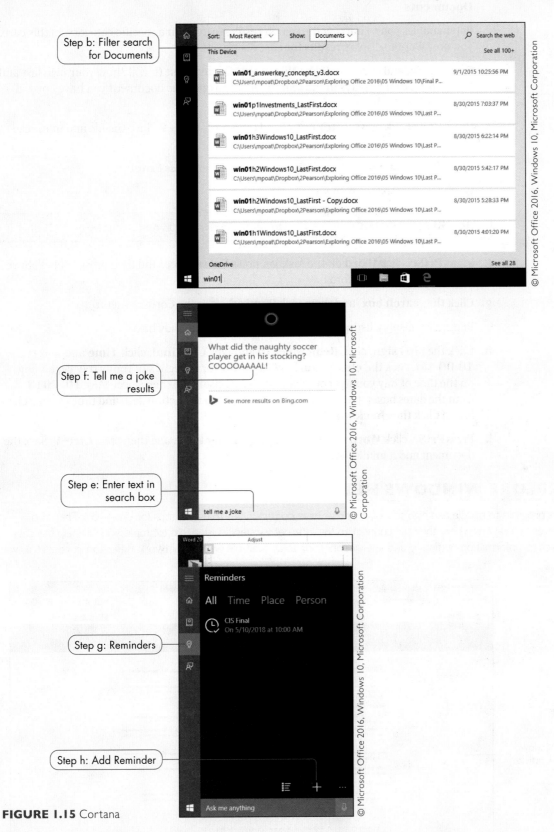

FIGURE 1.15 Cortana

a. Click the **search box**, and type **win**. Click **My stuff**.

A list of settings, applications, files, and folders that are stored on your PC that contain "win" in the name displays.

b. Click the **Sort arrow**, select **Most Recent**, click the **Show arrow**, and then select **Documents**.

Filter enables you to narrow the search results to items in a specific category. In this case, you only want to display results that are documents.

c. Press **PrtSc**, and click **win01h1Windows10_LastFirst** (it will show your own last and first names) that displays in the search results to open the document you have created with this Hands-On Exercise.

d. Press **Ctrl+End**, press **Enter** twice, and then press **Ctrl+V**. Save the file and minimize Word.

e. Click the **search box**, type **tell me a joke**, and then press **Enter**.

Cortana will display a response.

> **TROUBLESHOOTING:** You may need to initiate Cortana prior to completing Step e.

f. Press **PrtSc**, click **Word** on the taskbar, press **Enter** twice, and then press **Ctrl+V**. Save the file and minimize Word.

g. Click the **search box**, and then click **Reminders** in the Cortana menu.

Reminders display, listing any reminders you might already have.

h. Click the **plus sign**, click **Remember to** and type **CIS Final**, click **Time** and select **10:00 AM**, click the **check mark**, click **Today** (or it might say Tomorrow depending on the time of day you are completing this exercise), and then select **May 10, 2018** from the dates boxes. (Alternatively, you can put in the actual date and time of your class final.) Click the **check mark** again. Click **Remind**.

i. Press **PrtSc**, click **Word** on the taskbar, press **Enter** twice, and then press **Ctrl+V**. Save the document and minimize Word.

STEP 5 ›› **EXPLORE WINDOWS HELP**

As students in your class progress to middle and high school, they may have opportunities to use laptops for class work. They also are likely to find themselves in locations where they can connect to the Internet wirelessly. Using that example, you will help the class understand how to search for information on finding and safely connecting to an available wireless network. Refer to Figure 1.16 as you complete Step 5.

Step a: Windows Help Web link article

© Microsoft Office 2016, Windows 10, Microsoft Corporation

FIGURE 1.16 Windows Help

a. Click the **search box**, and type **Why use Windows Defender?** Press **Enter**. Select the Using Windows Defender – Windows Help Web link, and read the topic.

> **TROUBLESHOOTING:** If the webpage displays with a message, "Hi there - you're looking for Windows 10 info! We put that stuff in a new spot." click the arrow next to Windows 10 that displays next to the article title and select Windows 8.1, Windows RT 8.1. The information on Windows Defender is still applicable to Windows 10.

b. Click the **Start menu**, click the **Snipping Tool tile**, click the **New arrow**, and then select **Full-screen Snip**.

The Snipping Tool window displays with an image of your screen.

c. Click **Word** on the taskbar, press **Enter** twice, and then press **Ctrl+V**.

d. Press **Enter**, then, in your own words, type why you should use Windows Defender, and the two ways it helps protect your PC. Save the file. Minimize the Word and Snipping Tool windows.

e. Click the **search box** and type **File History help**. Press **Enter**. At the top of the Bing results, click **Videos**, and click **Restore files or folders using File History – Windows Help** link. Watch the video.

> **TROUBLESHOOTING:** If you can not locate this specific video, find and watch any video on File History from Microsoft.

f. Take a full-screen snip of your screen with the video information still displayed, click **Word** on the taskbar, press **Enter** twice, and then press **Ctrl+V**. Save the file.

g. Type **restore files** in the search box, and then click **Restore your files with File History – Control Panel**. Click **Snipping Tool** on the taskbar, click **New**, click the **New arrow**, and then click **Full-screen Snip**. Click **Word** on the taskbar, press **Enter** twice, and then press **Ctrl+V**.

h. Save the document. Keep the document open if you plan to continue with the next Hands-On Exercise. If not, close the document, and exit Word. Close all other windows.

File Management

One of the main functions of Windows 10 is *file management*, which provides an organizational structure to your computer's contents. Windows organizes the drives, folders, and files of your computer in a hierarchical structure. The hard drive is represented as the C: drive and is where most programs and files are permanently stored. A unique letter (D, E, F, and so on) identifies other storage devices, such as a DVD drive, external hard drive, or flash drive, when they are connected to the computer.

In this section, you will learn how to use File Explorer to manage your files and folders. You will also learn how to create a folder; then open, rename, and delete folders, so that you can better organize your files; and how to move or copy files between different folders. Lastly, you will learn how to compress and extract files and folders.

Using File Explorer

File Explorer is an app that you can use to create folders and manage folders and files across various storage locations: your PC, online storage, and external storage devices such as a flash drive or backup drive. File Explorer displays the organizational hierarchy of storage locations, folders, and files so you can locate files more easily. Often, related files are organized together into folders. A folder structure can occur across several levels, so you can create folders within other folders—called subfolders—arranged according to purpose. The most common analogy for File Explorer is that of a filing cabinet in which common documents and files are located within a single drawer (in this case a storage location), and then further grouped and organized by folders, often multiple layers of folders.

Understand the File Explorer Interface

Windows 10 has made it very easy to access File Explorer by incorporating an icon on the taskbar and in the Start menu. If you use File Explorer a lot, an icon will most likely also display in the Most used section of the Start menu.

Figure 1.17 shows and Table 1.1 further describes the various functional areas of the File Explorer interface.

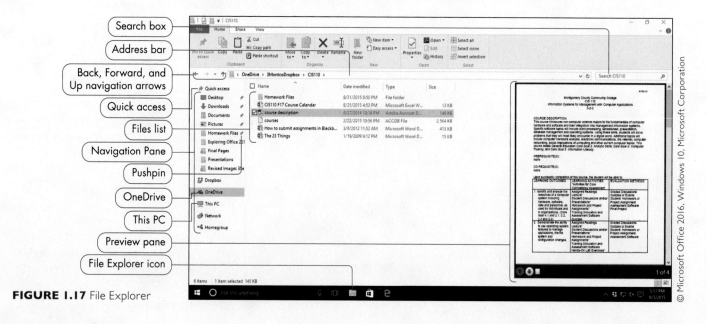

FIGURE 1.17 File Explorer

TABLE 1.1   File Explorer Interface

Ribbon	The Ribbon includes tabs and commands that are relevant to the currently selected item. If you are working with a music file, the Ribbon commands might include one for burning to a CD, whereas if you have selected a document, the Ribbon would enable you to open or share the file.
Back, Forward, and Up navigation arrows	Use these commands to visit previously opened folders. Use the Up command to open the parent folder for the current location.
Address bar	The Address bar enables you to navigate to other folders within File Explorer.
Search box	Find files and folders by typing descriptive text in the search box. Windows immediately begins a search after you type the first character, further narrowing results as you type. You can search the entire contents of File Explorer, or conduct a more directed search by first selecting a folder or drive.
Navigation Pane	The Navigation Pane contains Quick access, OneDrive, This PC, and Network. Click the arrow next to any of these content groups in the Navigation Pane to display contents and to manage files housed within a selected folder. Click any folder in the Navigation Pane to display the contained files.
Quick access	Quick access, as its name implies, provides immediate access to those files and folders that you use most often.
File list	The File list shows the contents of the currently selected folder or storage location. Files and folders can display in a variety of layouts that either show detailed information about the specific file or folder, or just file or folder names with small-, medium-, or large-sized icons. The icon is associated with the type of file or folder. For example, all Word documents will bear the W in a blue box icon.
Details pane	Displays the properties of the file or folder. Common properties include information such as the author name and the date the file was last modified. Details pane does not display by default, but displays after clicking the View tab and then clicking Details pane in the Panes group.
Preview pane	The Preview pane provides a snapshot of a selected file's contents (but not the contents of a selected folder). You can see file contents before actually opening the file. This pane can be displayed by clicking the View tab and then clicking Preview pane in the Panes group.

Use the View Tab on the Ribbon

File Explorer has a Ribbon, like all the Office applications. Use the View tab to customize what displays on File Explorer. For example, you might want to modify the size of the file and folder icons, or you might want additional details about displayed files and folders. Using the settings in the Layout group on the View tab, you can determine the size of icons by selecting Small, Medium, Large, or Extra Large icons. The Details layout will list the files and folder with other relevant information such as Date modified, Type, and Size. The List layout shows the file names without added detail, whereas Tiles and Content layouts are useful to show file thumbnails and varying levels of file details. If you want additional detail, such as who the file or folder is shared with and its availability, click Details pane on the View tab. To show a preview of a file, click Preview pane on the View tab. You can change the width of a pane by positioning the pointer on the border that separates the panes to display a double-headed arrow, and then dragging the border left or right.

Use and Modify Quick Access

When you launch File Explorer, it opens to the *Quick access* section on the Navigation Pane by default. Quick access contains shortcuts to the folders you use most often. Although certain folders such as Downloads, Desktop, Documents, and Pictures are pinned to Quick access by default, you can unpin any of those, and pin others, to meet your particular needs. A pushpin icon identifies a pinned folder (refer to Figure 1.17). If you have upgraded your system from Windows 7 or 8, all the folders in your Favorites list are added to Quick access automatically.

To pin a folder to Quick access, complete one of the following steps:

- Right-click the folder, and select Pin to (or Unpin from) Quick access.
- Select the folder to pin and then click Pin to Quick access on the Home tab. Clicking this button with a selected pinned folder does not unpin the folder, however.

Also displayed in Quick access is a list of Recent files. These files are the most frequently used files. As files are added, the less used files on the list are removed to make room for the new files, but you can remove any file from the Recent files list by right-clicking the file and selecting Remove from Quick access.

Use the Search Box in File Explorer

Occasionally, even the most organized person will need to search for a file or folder. While Cortana may be a convenient way to search for files and folders, you can only filter the results by type of file. When you use the search box in File Explorer, you can search only the contents of a specific folder, thus limiting the results; or you can Search an entire drive for a broader search. You can then further sort the results by file type or date modified to continue to locate the specific file or folder.

To search for a file or folder, complete the following steps:

1. Click the drive or folder in the Navigation Pane you want to search.
2. Type the search term in the search box.

Once you click in the File Explorer search box, the Search Tools tab displays. The Search Tools tab enables you to do the following:

- refine your search results by Date, Kind, Size, or Other properties
- revise the search location to include subfolders, the entire PC or another location
- save a search if you tend to conduct the same search repeatedly

Navigate File Explorer

The Navigation Pane is an easy way to move between folders and storage locations in File Explorer. As mentioned above, the Navigation Pane consists of four main areas: Quick access, OneDrive, This PC, and Network. *OneDrive* is Microsoft's cloud storage system.

Saving files to OneDrive, saves them to a Web-based location (OneDrive.com) and syncs them across all Windows devices. Sign in with your Microsoft account to access your files from any Internet-connected computer or mobile device. Changes you make will sync with the cloud, keeping your files up-to-date everywhere. Use File Explorer to access your OneDrive and to create new folders and organize existing folders.

TIP: CHOOSE WHAT TO SYNC

If you need to save space on your hard drive, sync just those OneDrive folders that you really use most often. The others are always available from OneDrive.com, but they will not show up in File Explorer. You can choose to sync everything in OneDrive or just certain folders or subfolders. Those folders or files you choose to sync will be added to your PC and to OneDrive so you can access them from other devices. Those folders or files you choose to stop syncing will not display in the OneDrive folder in File Explorer, but will remain in OneDrive and can be accessed from the OneDrive website. To choose which folders to sync, right-click the OneDrive icon in the Notification area on the taskbar. Then click Settings, click the Choose folders tab, and then click Choose folders. Uncheck those folders you do not want to sync and display in File Explorer. Only checked folders will sync.

Files stored to This PC are saved onto the hard drive, and are accessible only when working on that particular device. Documents, Music, Pictures, Videos, and Downloads are standard library folders in the This PC area of File Explorer. Clicking on Network in the Navigation Pane displays all networked devices such as gaming and entertainment systems, printers, and other networked computers.

Clicking the arrow on the left side of these main storage areas in the Navigation Pane expands or collapses the folder to show or hide the folders and documents within each group. When you select a file or folder, the location of that file or folder is displayed in the Address bar (see Figure 1.18).

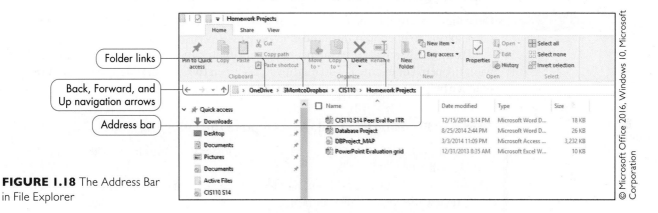

FIGURE 1.18 The Address Bar in File Explorer

The Address bar is located under the Ribbon, and displays the current location of a selected file or folder as a series of links and arrows. Next to the Address bar are the Back, Forward, and Up navigation arrows. These arrows help to move up or down the links in the location shown in the Address bar. Alternatively, you can click on any of the links in the Address bar to jump directly to the location. You can use the Address bar to navigate to a particular location (i.e., to Documents or Quick access), or you can click in any of the arrows between the folder links to view any subfolders. You can also use the Address bar to move files and folders to different locations. This and other ways to work with files and folders are covered in the next section.

Working with Files and Folders

STEP 1 ⟫⟩ As you work with software to create a file, such as when you type a report using Word, your primary concern will be saving the file so that you can retrieve it later. Grouping related files into folders helps to keep files organized. If you have created an appropriate and well-named folder structure, you can save the file in a location that is easy to find.

You can create a folder in a couple of different ways. You can use File Explorer to create a folder structure, providing descriptive names and placing the folders in a well-organized hierarchy.

To create a folder in File Explorer, complete the following steps:

1. Open File Explorer, and then click OneDrive or any other location such as the hard drive or flash drive, in the Navigation Pane.
2. Click the Home tab on the Ribbon, and then click New folder in the New group.
3. Type the new folder name and press Enter. Repeat the process to create additional folders.

Undoubtedly, you will occasionally find that you have just created a file but have no appropriate folder in which to save the file. For example, you might have just finished the slide show for your speech class but have forgotten first to create a speech folder for your assignments. For those occasions, you can create a folder from within the software application at the time you are saving a file.

To create a folder as you save a file, complete the following steps:

1. Click Save As in Backstage view and click Browse, to display the Save As dialog box.
2. Navigate to the location where you want to store your file.
3. Click New folder, type the new folder name, press Enter, and then click Open to save the name and open the new folder. After typing the file name, click Save.

Open, Rename, and Delete Folders and Files

 Once files are saved to locations such as OneDrive or Documents on This PC, you can use File Explorer to open, rename, and delete files.

Using the Navigation Pane or search box, you can locate and select a file that you want to open. For example, you might want to open the speech slide show so that you can practice before giving a presentation to the class.

To open a file using File Explorer, complete the following steps:

1. Open File Explorer, and then navigate to the folder that contains the desired file. The file will display in the File list.
2. Enable the Preview pane from the View tab, and click the file name in the File list to preview the contents of a file before opening it.
3. Double-click the file. The program that is associated with the file will open the file. For example, Microsoft PowerPoint will launch and a presentation will display when you double-click a file associated with PowerPoint.

At times, you may want to give a different name to a file or folder than the one that you originally gave it. Or perhaps you made a typographical mistake when you entered the name as you saved the file. In these situations, you can rename the file or folder.

To rename a file or folder, complete one of the following steps:

- Right-click the file or folder and select Rename. Type the new name and press Enter.
- Click the name twice—but much more slowly than a double-click. Type the new name and press Enter.
- Click a file or folder once to select it, click the Home tab, and then select Rename in the Organize group. Type the new name and press Enter.

It is much easier to delete a folder or file than it is to recover it if you remove it by mistake. Therefore, be very careful when deleting items so that you are sure of your intentions before proceeding. When you delete a folder, all subfolders and all files within the folder are also removed. If you are certain you want to remove a folder or file, the process is simple.

To delete a file or folder, complete one of the following steps:

- Right-click the item, click Delete, and then click Yes if asked to confirm removal to the Recycle Bin.
- Click to select the item, click the Home tab, and then click Delete in the Organize group.

Recall that items are placed in the Recycle Bin only if you are deleting them from a hard drive. Files and folders deleted from a removable storage medium, such as a flash drive, are immediately and permanently deleted, with no easy method of retrieval.

Selecting, Copying, and Moving Multiple Files and Folders

STEP 3 ▶▶ You will select folders and files when you need to rename, delete, copy, or paste them, or open files and folders so that you can view the contents. Click a file or folder to select it; double-click a file or folder (in the File list) to open it.

Select Multiple Files and Folders

To apply an operation to several files at once, such as deleting or moving them, you will select all of them. You can select several files and folders, regardless of whether they are adjacent to each other in the File list. Suppose that your digital pictures are contained in the Pictures folder. You might want to delete some of the pictures because you want to clear up some hard drive space.

To select multiple files or folders, complete the following steps:

1. Open File Explorer and click the desired folder or storage location.
2. Locate the desired files in the File list, and do one of the following:
   - Select the first file, press and hold Shift, and then click the last file to select adjacent files. All consecutive files will be highlighted, indicating that they are selected. At that point, you can delete, copy, or move the selected files at the same time.
   - Click the first file or folder, and press and hold Ctrl while you click all desired non-adjacent files or folders, releasing Ctrl only when you have finished selecting all the necessary files or folders. At that point, you can delete, copy, or move the selected files at the same time.
   - Open the folder, press and hold Ctrl, and then press A on the keyboard to select all items in a folder or disk drive. You can also click the Home tab, and in the Select group, click Select all to select all items. At that point, you can delete, copy, or move the selected files at the same time.

TIP: USING A CHECK BOX TO SELECT ITEMS
In Windows 10, it is easy to make multiple selections, even if the items are not adjacent. Open File Explorer, click the View tab and click to select Item check boxes in the Show/hide group. As you move the pointer along the left side of files and folders, a check box displays. Click the check box to select the file. If you want to select all items in the folder quickly, click the check box that displays in the Name column heading.

Copy and Move Files and Folders

When you copy or move a folder, you affect both the folder and any files that it contains. You can move or copy a folder or file to another location on the same drive or to another drive. If your purpose is to make a backup, or copy, of an important file or folder, you will probably want to copy it to an external drive or to OneDrive.

To move or copy an item in File Explorer, complete the following steps:

1. Right-click the item(s) and select either Cut (to move) or Copy on the shortcut menu.
2. Locate the destination drive or folder in the Navigation Pane, right-click the destination drive or folder, and then click Paste.

Compressing Files and Folders

 Sometimes you have an extremely large file, such as a video file that you want to email or upload to the Internet. Or, you might have a group of files, such as a bunch of pictures that you want to share with friends or family, but you do not want to send them as individual attachments. You can compress a file or zip multiple files together into a single compressed folder. A ***compressed (zipped) folder*** or file, takes up less space, is easier to email or to upload to OneDrive or another online storage site, and facilitates sharing a group of files.

Create a Compressed Folder

Using the Zip tool in File Explorer makes it easy to create a compressed folder. When compressing a file or folder, the compressed folder is created in the same location and takes on the same name as the file or folder. However, if you are compressing a group of files, it may be best to first put them in a folder and give that folder a meaningful name. Otherwise, the zipped folder will take the name of one of the documents in the folder. Of course, you can always rename a zipped folder, using the same methods described above for renaming a file or folder. The zipped file or folder does not replace the original files.

To compress a file or folder, complete the following series of steps:

1. Open File Explorer, and select the file, group of files, or folder in the File list that you want to compress.
2. Click the Share tab, and then click Zip in the Send group. A compressed folder is created and placed in the same folder location along with the original files or folder. Alternatively, right-click the selected files or folder, select Send to, and click Compressed (zipped) folder.

Once a compressed folder is created, you can add additional files to the folder without having to undo and redo the zipping process. Just drag new files into the compressed folder.

Extract Files from a Compressed Folder

You might have received or downloaded a compressed file or folder, such as the data files from this book, and need to unzip the folder and extract the files.

To unzip (extract) files or folders from a compressed folder, complete the following steps:

1. Open File Explorer, and select the compressed folder.

   This displays the Compressed Folder Tools tab.

2. Click the Extract tab, click Extract all, and if necessary, click Browse to select a destination where you want the individual files to be located. The individual files, by default, are saved to the same location as the zipped folder. Click Extract.

TIP: EXTRACTING FILES FROM A DOWNLOADED ZIP FOLDER

If you are extracting files from a folder you have downloaded from the Web, you should ensure your files are saved in a meaningful location. Otherwise, they may end up in the Downloads folder.

 Extracting files does not remove the compressed folder from your computer. The compressed folder will remain until you decide to delete it.

Quick Concepts

5. The File Explorer interface has several functional areas. Name them and identify their characteristics. ***pp. 24–25***

6. Describe why it might be more efficient to use the search box in File Explorer than the search box on the taskbar to look for a file. ***p. 26***

7. You want to delete several files, but the files are not consecutively listed in File Explorer. Describe two different methods you could use to select and delete them. ***p. 29***

8. Explain at least two circumstances in which file compression would be useful. ***p. 30***

Hands-On Exercises

 Watch the Video for This Hands-On Exercise!

 MyITLab® Topic-Based Training

Skills covered: Create Folders • Pin a Folder to Quick Access • Rename a Folder • Delete a Folder • Copy a File • Move a Folder • Compress a Folder • Extract Files from a Compressed Folder.

2 File Management

You have discussed with the students the importance of good file management, now you want to show them how easy it is to use File Explorer to organize and manage their files. You first have them create and pin a folder to Quick access, then you have them modify some folder names so they are more meaningful. Lastly, you show the students how to extract files from a compressed folder and move them to one of the previously created folders.

STEP 1 ❱❱ CREATE FOLDERS AND PIN A FOLDER TO QUICK ACCESS

Your friend tells you that she would like to have all the files the students are working on saved in one folder so it is easy for everyone to access in the future. Refer to Figure 1.19 as you complete Step 1.

Steps c and e: New folder

Step g: Pinned to Quick access

Steps c and g: OneDrive

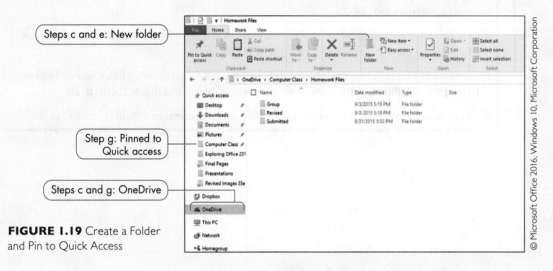

© Microsoft Office 2016, Windows 10, Microsoft Corporation

FIGURE 1.19 Create a Folder and Pin to Quick Access

a. Open *win01h1Windows10_LastFirst* if you closed it at the end of Hands-On Exercise 1 and save it as **win01h2Windows10_LastFirst**, changing h1 to h2. Keep the document open and maximized.

> **TROUBLESHOOTING:** If you make any major mistakes in this exercise, you can close the file, open *win01h1Windows10_LastFirst* again, and then start this exercise over.

b. Click **File Explorer** on the taskbar and maximize the window.

c. Click **OneDrive** in the Navigation Pane. Click **New folder** in the New group, type **Computer Class**, and then press **Enter**.

You create a folder where you can organize subfolders and files for the students and your friend, and all the learning materials they generate for their computer class.

> **TROUBLESHOOTING:** If OneDrive does not display in the Navigation Pane, click This PC and create a new folder in Documents.

> **TROUBLESHOOTING:** If the folder you create is called *New folder* instead of *Computer Class*, you probably clicked away from the folder before typing the name, so that it received the default name. To rename it, right-click the folder, click Rename, type the correct name, and then press Enter.

d. Double-click the **Computer Class folder** in the File list. The Address bar at the top of the File Explorer window should show that it is the currently selected folder.

e. Click **New folder** on the Home tab, in the New group, type **Data Files**, and then press **Enter**. Repeat the process to create another folder, and name it **Homework Files**.

You create two subfolders of the Computer Class folder. One to contain the data files the students will need to begin some of their computer work, and another to keep track of homework files they have completed.

f. Check the Address bar to make sure Computer Class is still the current folder. Navigate to and then double-click the **Homework Files folder** in the Navigation Pane. Right-click in a blank area of the File list, point to **New**, and then click **Folder**. Type **Submitted** and press **Enter**. Using either technique in this step, create two more folders named **Group** and **Revised**.

To subdivide the Homework Files folder further, you create three subfolders, one to hold homework files that have been submitted, one for revised homework files, and one for homework files from group projects.

g. Click **OneDrive** in the Navigation Pane, and locate the Computer Class folder in the File list. Right-click the **Computer Class folder**, and select **Pin to Quick access**.

The Computer Class folder displays in the Quick access area of File Explorer.

h. Double-click the **Computer Class folder** in Quick access, and double-click the **Homework Files folder** in the Files list.

i. Click **Snipping Tool** on the taskbar, click the **New arrow**, and click **Full-screen Snip**. Click **Word** on the taskbar, press **Ctrl+End**, press **Enter** twice, and then press **Ctrl+V**.

j. Save the document. Minimize the Word and Snipping Tool windows.

TROUBLESHOOTING: If the Snipping Tool does not display on the taskbar, open the Start menu, and click the Snipping Tool tile to launch the app.

STEP 2 ❯❯ **RENAME AND DELETE A FOLDER**

As often happens, you find that the folder structure you created is not exactly what you need. You will remove the Revised folder and will rename the Data Files folder to better describe the contents. Refer to Figure 1.20 as you complete Step 2.

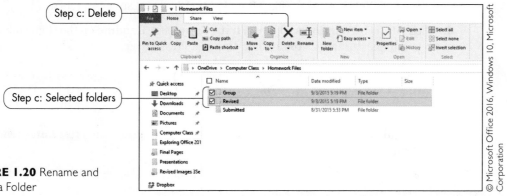

FIGURE 1.20 Rename and Delete a Folder

a. Double-click the **Computer Class folder** in Quick access.

b. Right-click the **Data Files folder**, click **Rename**, type **Starting Files**, and then press **Enter**.

Your friend thinks that her students will understand the term Starting Files better than Data Files, so you rename the folder.

c. Double-click the **Homework Files folder**. Click the check box next to **Revised** and **Group**. Both folders are selected. Click **Delete** in the Organize group. If asked to confirm the deletion, click **Yes**. Click **Computer Class** in the Address bar.

> **TROUBLESHOOTING:** If check boxes do not display next to the folder name, click the View tab, and click to select *Item check boxes* in the Show/hide group.

You decide that dividing the homework folder into revised and group subfolders is not necessary, so you deleted both folders.

d. Take a full-screen snip of your screen, click **Word** on the taskbar, press **Enter** twice, and then press **Ctrl+V**.

e. Save the document. Minimize the Word and Snipping Tool windows.

STEP 3)) SELECT AND COPY FILES

You want to show students how to copy a file, so in anticipation of completing the next assignment, you have them copy and rename the current homework file they are working on. Refer to Figure 1.21 as you complete Step 3.

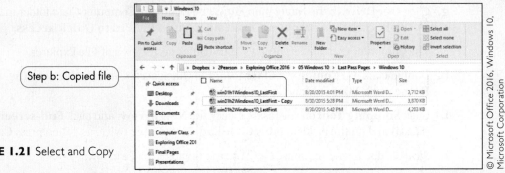

Step b: Copied file

FIGURE 1.21 Select and Copy Files

© Microsoft Office 2016, Windows 10, Microsoft Corporation

a. Navigate to the location where you saved *win01h2Windows10_LastFirst*. Right-click the file and select **Copy**.

b. Right-click in a **blank area** of the File list and select **Paste**.

A new document named win01h2Windows10_LastFirst - Copy displays. Two documents with the same name cannot be saved in the same location, so Windows automatically adds "- Copy" to the end of the file name to differentiate the two files.

c. Take a full-screen snip of your screen, click **Word** on the taskbar, press **Enter** twice, and then press **Ctrl+V**. Save the file. Minimize the Word and Snipping Tool windows.

d. Click **win01h2Windows10_LastFirst - Copy**, click **Rename** on the Home tab, and then rename the file as **Homework_Images**. Press **Enter**.

> **TROUBLESHOOTING:** Be sure the file you are renaming has - Copy in the file name.

e. Take a full-screen snip of your screen, click **Word** on the taskbar, press **Enter** twice, and then press **Ctrl+V**.

f. Save the document. Minimize the Word and Snipping Tool windows.

You want to show the students how to compress a group of files into a zipped folder and then move the zipped folder to a new location. You will then have the students extract the files from the zipped folder. Refer to Figure 1.22 as you complete Step 4.

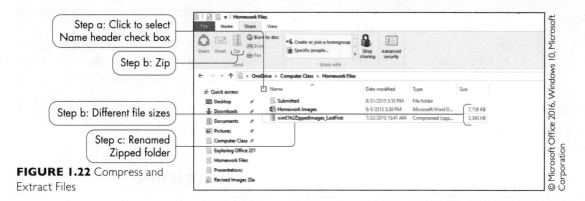

FIGURE 1.22 Compress and Extract Files

a. Click the **check box** next to the Name header in the File list in File Explorer to select all three documents.

> **TROUBLESHOOTING:** If more than the three documents display in the File list, click the check box to select each individual file.

b. Click the **Share tab**, click **Zip**, and then press **Enter**.

A new zipped folder is created. Because the files were not in a separate folder, the zipped folder is named after one of the files. You will to rename the zipped folder.

c. Right-click the **zipped folder**, and click **Rename**. Type **Windows 10 Homework**, and press **Enter**.

d. Click the **Windows 10 Homework zipped folder**, press **Ctrl**, and then drag the folder to the Computer Class folder in Quick access.

A ScreenTip will display Copy to Computer Class. Note: If you wanted to move the zipped folder, you would just drag the folder to the new location.

e. Double-click the **Computer Class folder** in Quick access, and then double-click the **Windows 10 Homework zipped folder**.

The Compressed Folder Tools tab displays on the Ribbon, and the three files contained in the zipped folder display in the File list.

f. Take a full-screen snip of your screen, click **Word** on the taskbar, press **Enter** twice, and then press **Ctrl+V**. Save the file. Minimize the Word and Snipping Tool windows.

g. Click **Extract all**, and then click **Extract**.

You do not need to browse, as you want the new files to stay in the Computer Class folder.

h. Click **Computer Class** on the Address bar and note that the Windows 10 Homework zipped folder and the Windows 10 Homework folder are both in the Computer Class folder.

i. Take a full-screen snip of your screen, click **Word** on the taskbar, press **Enter** twice, and then press **Ctrl+V**. Close the Snipping Tool and close File Explorer. Click **No** if asked to save changes to the snip.

j. Save the document. Keep the document open if you plan to continue with the next Hands-On Exercise. If not, close the document, and exit Word. Close all other windows.

Windows System and Security Features

Windows 10 is a full-featured operating system. As such, it includes utilities that help to monitor, maintain, and secure your devices. Windows 10 contains software that protects your system against spyware and hacking, as well as utilities that help to keep your system up-to-date or recover files should something go awry. It also includes some maintenance utilities to ensure your computer and operating system continue to run in good form.

In this section, you will learn about some maintenance and security features in Windows 10.

Working with Security Settings and Software

Windows 10 monitors your security status, providing recommendations for security settings and software updates as needed. The Action Center provides a central location where you can access any status notifications and alerts. Windows 10 includes basic security features such as Window Defender and firewall software.

Understand the Action Center

STEP 1 Windows 10 monitors your system for various maintenance and security settings, providing notifications and recommending action through the ***Action Center*** when necessary. A major purpose of the Action Center is to provide important status information. Status information could include the detection of new devices, the availability of software updates, or recommended maintenance and security tasks. When the status of a monitored item changes, a pop-up message in an alert box displays near the Notification area. You can click the message to perform the recommended task. If you are not working on your computer at the time the pop-up message appears, the Action Center icon, located in the Notification area of the taskbar, will turn opaque indicating that there are new notifications waiting for you. Click the Action Center icon in the Notification area (see Figure 1.23) to display the Action Center alerts box. Once clicked, the Action Center icon will become clear or "empty."

Notifications area in Action Center

Action Center icon

Quick actions buttons

FIGURE 1.23 Action Center

The Action Center consists of two parts: the Notifications area at the top and Quick actions buttons at the bottom (refer to Figure 1.23). The Action Center runs across all your Windows devices. Therefore, in the Notifications area, you will see notifications from various apps, including Facebook, Twitter, and your email account, as well as from apps that might only be on your Windows phone or tablet. You can delete notifications by group (i.e. all your Twitter notifications) or you can delete individual notifications by pointing to the group or individual notification name and then clicking the "X" that displays. Lastly, you can click Clear All at the top of the Notifications area. Be mindful that Clear All will delete all notifications on all your Windows devices, not just the device on which you are currently working.

In the bottom of the Action Center are quick action buttons such as a Tablet mode toggle button, a button to connect your media devices, a link to All settings, a link to the Display settings, and toggle buttons for Location and Wi-Fi. Click Expand to see more quick actions such as toggle buttons for VPN and Rotation lock. Note that some buttons, such as Airplane mode or Rotation lock, will only display on mobile devices.

To change the quick action buttons in the Action Center, complete the following steps:

1. Click the All settings button in the Action Center (or click Settings from the Start menu).
2. Click System, and then Notifications & actions. In the Quick actions area (see Figure 1.24), four icons display, indicating the quick actions that will display in the Action Center.
3. Click any of the icons to change any or all of the actions, and then select another action from the displayed menu.

Also from the Notifications & actions menu, you can choose which icons will always display in the Notification area on the taskbar by clicking *Select which icons appear on the taskbar*.

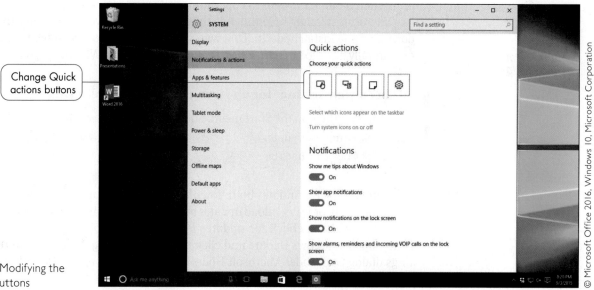

FIGURE 1.24 Modifying the Quick Actions Buttons

Use File History

Many things can accidently happen to your files. You might mistakenly delete a file or a file might become corrupted, meaning it is damaged and therefore unusable by your software programs. Windows **File History** is a utility that will continuously make copies of your important files so that you can recover them if you ever encounter a file problem. In order for you to take advantage of the File History feature, you need to ensure that File History is turned on and that a storage area, such as a separate partition of your hard drive, an external drive, or cloud storage such as OneDrive, has been selected as the back-up location.

To access File History, complete the following steps:

1. Right-click Start, and select Control Panel.
2. Select System and Security, and then click File History.

File History will save files to a drive that you designate, such as an external hard drive or a separate partition (section) of your computer's internal hard drive. To set up File History for the first time, you must first designate the drive where File History will store the file backups. Click *Select drive* in the File History window to see a list of drives connected to your computer. If you need to set up a drive, click *Add network location*. Once you have selected a drive, click the *Run now* link to back up your files. As long as File History is on, it will automatically back up your personal files on your PC. If there are some folders that you do not feel need backing up, such as the Downloads folder, you can exclude them by clicking Exclude folders. Click Advanced settings to choose how often you want the backup to run and how long your saved versions are kept.

If you want to restore files after one or more have been lost, you can use the Restore feature in File History. Unlike many other restore applications, once you begin the restore process, you can browse to a specific file or folder and see all versions of the selected folder or individual file. You can then navigate to the desired version by clicking on Previous or Next and click Restore to bring it back to its original location.

Access Windows Update

Microsoft constantly identifies ways to enhance Windows security or fix problems that occur. There is no need to download or purchase an updated operating system each time changes are necessary; instead, you can simply make sure that your computer is set to download automatically any updates (fixes). **Windows Update** provides a means to initiating such modifications to the operating system.

Microsoft strongly recommends that you configure your computer to automatically download and install updates. That way, you do not have to remember to check for updates or manually download them. This is the default setting for Windows Update in Windows 10.

To check your settings for updates, complete the following steps:

1. Select Settings on the Start menu, and click Update & security.
2. Click Windows Update.
3. Click Check for updates.

You can have Windows both download and install updates automatically (strongly recommended), only download updates but let you install them, or never check for updates.

If you want to check for updates for other Microsoft products, such as Microsoft Office, open Windows Update and click the *Change settings* link. Then in the Change settings dialog box, under Microsoft Update, check *Give me updates for other Microsoft products when I update Windows*.

Use Windows Defender

Viruses and spyware can be installed on your computer without your knowledge when you connect to the Internet, open an email message, or when you install certain apps using a flash drive or other removable media. Spyware and viruses can do many unpleasant things such as:

- Keep track of websites you visit
- Change browser settings to direct you to dangerous websites

- Record keystrokes for stealing sensitive information
- Erase or corrupt files on your hard drive

Obviously, viruses and spyware are unwelcome and potential security risks. **Windows Defender** is antispyware and antivirus software. It identifies and removes malware such as viruses and spyware. Windows Defender can be set to run with real-time protection, which means that it is always on to guard against threats, alerting you when malicious programs attempt to install themselves or change your computer settings. You can also schedule routine scans so that Windows Defender checks your system for malicious software.

To open Windows Defender, complete the following steps:

1. Open the Start menu, and click All apps.
2. Click Windows System, and then click Windows Defender.

Alternatively, type Defender in the search box, and then click the corresponding link at the top of the Results list. This opens up the Windows Defender dialog box, and from there you can determine the type of Scan (Quick, Full, Custom).

Use Windows Firewall

STEP 2 ⟩⟩ Windows 10 also includes a **firewall**, a software program that helps to protect against unauthorized access (hacking) to your computer. Although Windows Defender and Windows Firewall provide basic protection, many computer users opt for the purchase of third-party software, such as Norton Internet Security, to provide an even greater level of protection.

When you work with the Internet, there is always a possibility that a hacker could disable your computer or view its contents. To keep that from occurring, it is imperative that you use firewall software. Windows 10 includes firewall software that is turned on by default when the operating system is installed. It protects against unauthorized traffic, both incoming and outgoing. That means that other people, computers, or programs do not have authorization to communicate with your computer unless you give permission. In addition, programs on your system are unable to communicate online unless you approve them.

Periodically, you might want to check to make sure your firewall has not been turned off accidentally. If you have another security program installed, such as Norton Internet Security, it has its own firewall software and therefore may recommend that Windows Firewall be turned off. This is because two active firewall programs can sometimes interfere with each other. But you should ensure that one firewall program is turned on at all times.

To access Windows Firewall, complete the following steps:

1. Open the Start menu, and then click Settings.
2. Type Firewall in Settings search box, and then click Windows Firewall.

   Alternatively, type Firewall in the search box, and select the top box in the search results.
3. Click Turn Windows Firewall on or off. You can then adjust other Firewall settings. Table 1.2 describes the Firewall settings that can be customized.

TABLE 1.2 Microsoft Firewall Settings

Setting	Description
Turn on Windows Firewall	Selected to be on by default to block most apps from receiving information through the firewall. You can add an app to a list of allowable apps.
Block all incoming connections	This setting, when turned on, blocks all unsolicited attempts to connect to your PC, even from those allowed apps. Consider turning this on when you are working in public places such as the airport or hotel. Turning this on does not affect your ability to use email and view most webpages.
Notify me when Windows Firewall blocks a new app	Selecting this option will allow you to unblock an app the Firewall has blocked.
Turn off Windows Firewall (not recommended)	Turn off Windows Firewall only if you have a separate security program, such as Norton or McAfee, running on your PC.

Working with Administrative Tools

One of the functions of the operating system is to manage computer resources such as the central processing unit (CPU) and random access memory (RAM). It is useful to have a good understanding of how well the CPU, RAM, and other computer resources are working so you can take preventative actions, such as upgrading the amount of RAM in your system, or freeing up or acquiring more hard drive capacity, if necessary. Windows 10 provides some tools that can help you monitor computer resources.

Use Task Manager

Task Manager displays the programs and processes that are running on your computer. When a program is not responding, you can use Task Manager to close it.

To close a program that is not responding, complete the following steps:

1. Right-click the taskbar, right-click the Start button, or use the search box to find Task Manager.
2. Click More details, click the Processes tab, and then click the application that is not responding in the Apps section.
3. Click End task.

To view how the computer is performing, click the Performance tab. Leave this box open as you work, so you can see how your actions affect computer resources.

Monitor System Resources

The **Resource Monitor** displays how the computer is using its key components, including the CPU and RAM. Use the search box to access the Resource Monitor, or click the Windows Administrative Tools folder in All apps. By clicking on each tab in the Resource Monitor window, you can view in real-time the system resources as they are being used. For example, click the Memory tab to view how RAM is being used (see Figure 1.25). The chart at the bottom displays the total amount of memory installed, what is currently being used, what is on reserve (cached), and what is currently available. Click between CPU and Memory to view how your actions affect the utilization of these components. For example, as you work, if the CPU performance nears or exceeds 50% utilization, that means you are using most or all of the CPU's capabilities. At maximum, or near maximum utilization, your computer might not run as efficiently. Unfortunately, there is not an easy way to upgrade your CPU, so if you want greater performance, it might be time to get a new computer with a faster CPU. You can also monitor memory

(RAM) utilization. If you find you are using most of your memory resources, it might be possible to add additional RAM to your computer. If you cannot add additional RAM, then again, it might be time for a computer that offers greater RAM capacity.

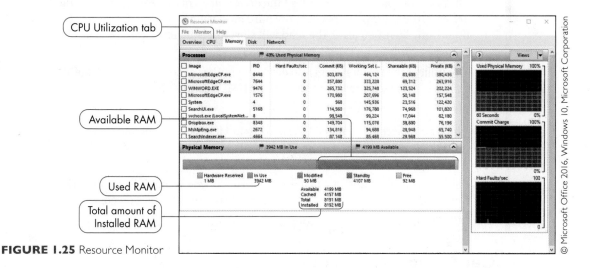

CPU Utilization tab

Available RAM

Used RAM

Total amount of Installed RAM

FIGURE 1.25 Resource Monitor

Use Disk Cleanup

STEP 3 Every now and then it is a good idea to do some internal "spring cleaning" on your computer. Over time, your computer system can accumulate many unnecessary files and program fragments that ultimately end up affecting computer performance. Some of these files accumulate in the Recycle Bin. Recall that deleted files from the hard disk go to the Recycle Bin but are not completely deleted from the system until the Recycle Bin is emptied. Windows often creates temporary files that temporarily store data. Usually Windows deletes these files automatically, but some remain. There are also files in Downloads that are not necessary anymore, such as small plug-ins and applets; or there are temporary files created when you use the Internet. The **Disk Cleanup** tool helps to free up space on your hard drive by searching for, and removing, any or all of these unnecessary files (see Figure 1.26).

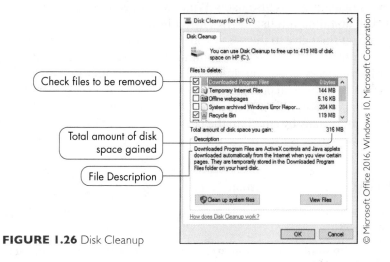

Check files to be removed

Total amount of disk space gained

File Description

FIGURE 1.26 Disk Cleanup

To run Disk Cleanup, complete the following steps:

1. Click All apps from the Start menu, and click Windows Administrative Tools.

2. Click Disk Cleanup, and then select the drive you want to clean up by clicking the arrow in the Drives box. To clean the hard disk, choose the (C:) drive. Click OK. Note: If you only have one drive, the scan will start immediately without the need to select a drive.

   The utility scans your system and displays another dialog box with a list of items that can be selected to be removed (or kept) by Disk Cleanup.

3. Click the check boxes by all of the items you want to remove to select them.

   When you select an item, read the description if you do not understand what the files are. For additional information, you can click View files to see a list of the files that will be deleted.

4. Click OK after selecting all the file categories that you want to delete, and then click Delete Files to confirm that you want to delete the selected file categories.

   Disk Cleanup will display the total amount of disk space gained by deleting the files.

Get Remote Assistance

Undoubtedly, you will have trouble with your computer at some time and need some assistance. You might consider getting someone to help you by letting him or her connect to your computer remotely to determine the problem. Of course, you will only want to ask someone that you trust because that person will temporarily have access to your files.

To allow Remote Assistance in Windows 10, complete the following steps:

1. Type Remote Access in the search box, and press Enter.

   The System Properties dialog box displays with the Remote tab selected.

2. Ensure that the Allow Remote Assistance connections to this computer check box is selected.

If the person who is helping you is also using Windows 10, you can use a method called Easy Connect. The first time you use Easy Connect to request assistance, you will receive a password that you then give to the person offering assistance. Using that password, the helper can remotely connect to your computer and exchange information. Thereafter, a password is not necessary—you simply click the contact information for the helper to initiate a session. If the person providing assistance is using an earlier Windows operating system (such as Windows 8.1), you can use an invitation file, which is a file that you create that is sent (usually by email) to the person offering assistance. The invitation file includes a password that is used to connect the two computers.

Quick Concepts

9. Describe the Action Center and the function it serves. **pp. 36–37**

10. Describe why you might use File History, and how it differs from other restore applications. **pp. 37–38**

11. Describe the utilities you would use to monitor and manage computer resources, such as the CPU and RAM. **pp. 40–41**

12. Describe the types of files that can be removed with Disk Cleanup. **p. 41**

Hands-On Exercise

Watch the Video
for This Hands-On
Exercise!

MyITLab®
Topic-Based
Training

Skills covered: Use the Action Center • Modify Firewall Settings • Use Disk Cleanup

3 Windows System and Security Features

Windows is a gateway to using application software. You know that the fifth-grade students are most interested in the fun things that can be done with software. You want to excite them about having fun with a computer, but you also want them to understand that along with the fun comes some need to maintain the computer. They also need to understand the concerns about security and privacy. You also want the students to be confident in their ability but well aware that help is available when they need it. In this section of your demonstration, you will encourage them to understand how they can perform some basic maintenance tasks. You will also show them features in Windows that can help address security concerns. Lastly, you will show them how easy it is to get help should they need assistance or reminders of how to work with Windows.

STEP 1 ⟫ USE THE ACTION CENTER

The Action Center will occasionally display messages regarding security and privacy settings. You want the Cedar Grove students to be aware of how important those messages are, so you will show them how to use the Action Center. Refer to Figure 1.27 as you complete Step 1.

> **TROUBLESHOOTING:** If you are working in a campus lab, you might not have access to the Action Center or Windows Update. In that case, you should skip this Hands-On Exercise.

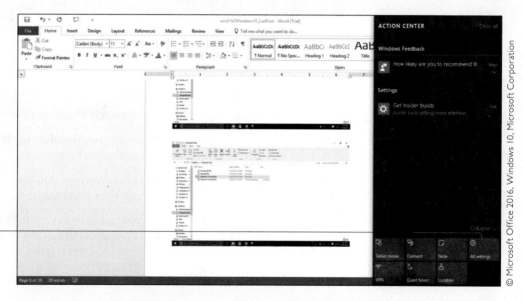

Step d: All Settings

FIGURE 1.27 The Action Center

© Microsoft Office 2016, Windows 10, Microsoft Corporation

a. Open *win01h2Windows10_LastFirst* if you closed it at the end of Hands-On Exercise 2 and save it as **win01h3Windows10_LastFirst**, changing h2 to h3. Keep the document open and maximized.

b. Click **Action Center** in the Notification area on the taskbar.

Although any alerts displayed on your computer may vary from those shown in Figure 1.27, the general appearance should be similar.

c. Press **PtrSc**, click **Word** on the taskbar, press **Ctrl+End**, press **Enter** twice, and then press **Ctrl+V**. Save the file. Minimize Word.

d. Click **Action center**, click **All settings**, click **System**, and then click **Notifications & actions**. Press **PtrSc**, click **Word** on the taskbar, press **Enter** twice, and then press **Ctrl+V**. Save the file. Minimize Word.

e. Click the **Back arrow** in the upper left of the Settings window, and then click **Update & security**.

Windows Update displays.

f. Click **Check for updates**.

g. Press **PtrSc**, click **Word** on the taskbar, press **Enter** twice, and then press **Ctrl+V**. Save the document. Minimize Word and close the Settings window.

STEP 2 ›› **MODIFY FIREWALL SETTINGS**

Although you do not expect the students to understand completely how firewalls work, you do want them to know that Windows includes a firewall and that they can manage firewall settings. Refer to Figure 1.28 as you complete Step 2.

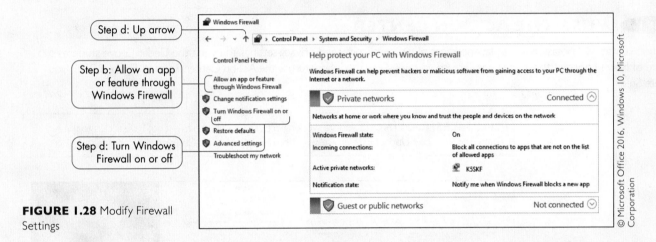

FIGURE 1.28 Modify Firewall Settings

a. Type **Firewall** in the search box, and then select **Windows Firewall - Control Panel**.

b. Click **Allow an App or feature through Windows Firewall**.

c. Take a full-screen snip of your screen, click **Word** on the taskbar, press **Enter** twice, and then press **Ctrl+V**. Minimize Word and the Snipping Tool windows.

d. Click the **up arrow** to return to main screen of Windows Firewall, and click **Turn Windows Firewall on or off**. Note the checkmarks.

e. Take a full-screen snip of your screen, click **Word** on the taskbar, press **Enter** twice, and then press **Ctrl+V**. Save the document. Minimize the Word and the Snipping Tool windows.

f. Click **Cancel**, and then close the Windows Firewall window.

You want to stress how important it is to run routine maintenance tasks on the computer. In addition to periodically wiping down the keyboard and monitor, you tell the students they should run the Disk Cleanup utility to remove unnecessary files that have accumulated. Refer to Figure 1.29 as you complete Step 3.

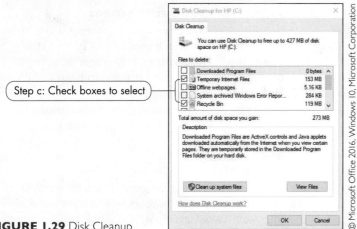

Step c: Check boxes to select

FIGURE 1.29 Disk Cleanup

a. Open the **Start** menu, click **All apps**, and then click **Windows Administrative Tools**. Click **Disk Cleanup**.

b. Ensure drive C: displays in the Disk cleanup: Drive Selection dialog box, and click **OK**.

   Disk Cleanup scans the hard disk drive for any unnecessary files that can be removed.

c. Click the check boxes to select **Recycle Bin** and **Temporary Internet Files** in the Files to delete section. Click to deselect any other check marks.

d. Take a full-screen snip of your screen, click **Word** on the taskbar, press **Enter** twice, and then press **Ctrl+V**. Save the file.

e. Click **Disk Cleanup** on the taskbar, and then click **OK**. Click **Delete Files** when asked are you sure you want to permanently delete these files. Right-click **Snipping Tool** on the taskbar, and click **Close window**. Do not save changes.

f. Save and close the file. Based on your instructor's directions, submit win01h3Windows10_LastFirst.

Chapter Objectives Review

After reading this chapter, you have accomplished the following objectives:

1. Understand the Windows 10 Interface

- Sign in to a Microsoft Account: A Microsoft account is necessary to use any Microsoft Services, including logging into Windows 10.
- Access Sleep and Power settings: Windows will go to sleep, a power-saving state, after a pre-determined period of inactivity. Restarting the computer is a warm boot. To power down the computer completely, choose Shut down.
- Explore the Windows 10 Start menu: The desktop is the primary working area that displays when you log into Windows. The Start menu is accessed by clicking the Start button on the taskbar. The Start menu has program tiles that can be arranged in groups, a Most used list of frequently used programs, and access to File Explorer, Documents, Settings, and Power. Clicking All apps changes the left panel of the Start menu to a list of all programs installed on the device.
- Configure the Start Menu: You can easily add and remove tiles from the Windows 10 Start menu. Adding a tile to the Start menu or an icon to the taskbar is known as pinning. You can organize the tiles into groups by dragging them around the screen. You can also assign appropriate names for each group of tiles. Tiles can be resized and removed from the Start menu.
- Explore the taskbar: The taskbar displays icons of open programs, as well as Start, the search box, and the Notification area. A Task View enables you to view all current tasks in one glance. Frequently used programs can be pinned to the taskbar. Right-clicking an open program icon on the taskbar opens a Jump List.
- Identify desktop components: On the desktop, icons represent links to programs, files, folder, or other items related to your computer. The Recycle Bin is temporary storage for deleted files. Shortcuts are icons to program files.
- Customize the desktop: You can customize the desktop with a different background color or theme.

2. Manage and Use the Desktop and Components

- Use Task View: Task View enables you to see all open windows, and to organize them into separate workspaces.
- Create a virtual desktop: Virtual desktops help to organize and access groups of windows for different purposes.
- Identify windows components: Windows can be moved, resized, stacked, or snapped into position so that multiple windows are easier to work with and identify.
- Snap, move, and resize windows: You can display up to four Windows 10 apps at a time using Snap and Snap Assist. Dialog boxes are windows that display when a program requires user interaction.

3. Use Windows 10 Search Features

- Use the search box: A search box, incorporated into the taskbar for easy access, is used to search the Web and the device. If you are looking for help or specific answers, you can type search keyword(s) in the search box and then click any resulting links.
- Use Cortana: When enabled, Cortana, Microsoft's personal assistant, can assist with tasks such as reminders and directions, provide a news feed, as well as search the Web and the device. Cortana's settings are managed through the Cortana Notebook.
- Get help: Cortana and the search box are the primary resources for help and support for Windows and other Microsoft-related questions.
- Manage the Cortana Notebook and settings: You can add or modify your preferences in Cortana Notebook. As you use Cortana, she will adapt to your preferences and be able to better predict your needs.

4. Use File Explorer

- File Explorer is an app used to create and manage folders and files across various storage locations on your PC, online storage, external storage, and networks.
- Understand the File Explorer interface: File Explorer displays the organizational hierarchy of storage locations, folders, and files.
- Use the View tab on the Ribbon: The View tab contains controls that manage how files and folders are displayed in File Explorer.
- Use and modify Quick access: Quick access is a new feature of File Explorer that contains shortcuts to folders you use most often. Folders can be pinned and removed from Quick access.
- Use the search box in File Explorer: Use the search box in File Explorer to search for specific files and folders. Results can be filtered by type, date modified, or other properties for further search refinement.
- Navigate File Explorer: The Navigation Pane is used to move between folders and storage locations. Clicking next to each main area in the Navigation Pane expands or collapses the folder to show or hide contents.
- Working with files and folders: Grouping related files into folders helps keep them organized and easier to locate.
- Open, rename, and delete folders and files: Click on a file or folder to open it, right-click and select Rename to give the folder or file a different name, right-click and select Delete to remove the file or folder from File Explorer.

5. Select, Copy, and Move Multiple Files and Folders

- Select multiple files and folders: Select adjacent files while pressing the Shift key. Select non-adjacent files while pressing the Ctrl key. Alternatively, click the check box next to each item to select.
- Copy and move file and folders: Files and folders can be copied and moved by dragging to a new location, as needed.

6. Compress Files and Folders

- Create a compressed folder: Compress a folder or a group of files using the Zip tool to facilitate sending a large file or a group of files using email or uploading to the Web.
- Extract files from a compressed folder: To unzip, use the the Extract all feature on the Extract tab.

7. Work with Security Settings and Software

- Understand the Action Center: The Action Center monitors the status of your security and maintenance settings, alerting you when maintenance tasks (such as backing up your system) are overlooked or when your security is at risk (for example, when antivirus software is out of date).
- Use File History: The File History utility can be configured to automatically make backups of your important files while you work.

- Access Windows Update: Windows Update provides a means to push modifications and fixes made to the operating system to the computer.
- Use Windows Defender: Windows Defender, an antivirus and antispyware program, is included with Windows and works to identify and remove malicious software.
- Use Windows firewall: A Windows firewall protects against unauthorized access to your computer from outside entities and prohibits unauthorized programs from accessing your computer without your permission.

8. Work with Administrative Tools

- Use Task Manager: Task Manager displays programs and processes that are running on your computer. Task Manager can be used to close a program when it is not responding.
- Monitor system resources: Resource Monitor displays how the computer is using its key components, including the CPU and RAM.
- Use Disk Cleanup: Disk Cleanup is used to remove unnecessary files from the computer that can slow down system performance.
- Get remote assistance: Remote assistance allows a third party to take control of your device.

Key Terms Matching

Match the key terms with their definitions. Write the key term letter by the appropriate numbered definition.

a. Action Center
b. Compressed (zipped) folder
c. Cortana
d. Desktop
e. Disk Cleanup
f. File Explorer
g. File History
h. File management
i. Notification area
j. OneDrive

k. Pin
l. Quick access
m. Search box
n. Start menu
o. Task Manager
p. Task View
q. Taskbar
r. Tile
s. Virtual desktop
t. Windows Defender

1. _____ An administrative tool in Windows that is used to remove unnecessary files from the computer. **p. 41**

2. _____ Primary working area of Windows 10. **p. 5**

3. _____ A utility in Windows that continuously makes copies of your important files so that you can recover them if you encounter a file problem. **p. 37**

4. _____ Microsoft's cloud storage system. **p. 26**

5. _____ A folder that uses less drive space and can be transferred or shared with other users more quickly. **p. 30**

6. _____ A component of File Explorer that contains shortcuts to the most frequently used folders. **p. 26**

7. _____ The main access to all programs and features on your computer. **p. 5**

8. _____ The Windows 10 personal assistant that helps search the Web and your PC, and can also assist with reminders, tasks, and other activities. **p. 15**

9. _____ The means of providing an organizational structure to file and folders. **p. 24**

10. _____ Detects and removes viruses and spyware. **p. 39**

11. _____ Displays the programs and processes that are running on your computer. It is also used to close a non-responding program. **p. 40**

12. _____ Located on the taskbar, provides a convenient way to search your computer or the Web. **p. 7**

13. _____ Provides status information, notifications, and recommended actions for various maintenance and security settings. **p. 36**

14. _____ Horizontal bar at the bottom of the desktop that displays open applications, the Notification area, the search box, and pinned apps or programs. **p. 7**

15. _____ Provides system status alerts in pop-up boxes. **p. 7**

16. _____ A process to add a tile to the Start menu or an icon to the taskbar. **p. 6**

17. _____ A block icon on the Start menu that represents a program or app. **p. 6**

18. _____ A way to organize and access groups of windows for different purposes. **p. 11**

19. _____ The Windows app that is used to create folders and manage files and folders across various storage locations. **p. 24**

20. _____ Feature on the taskbar that enables the user to view thumbnail previews of all open tasks in one glance. **p. 11**

Multiple Choice

1. The Windows 10 feature that alerts you to any maintenance or security concerns is the:

   (a) Action Center.

   (b) Security Center.

   (c) Windows Defender.

   (d) Control Panel.

2. Snapping apps means that you:

   (a) Minimize all open apps simultaneously so that the Start menu displays.

   (b) Auto arrange all open apps so that they are of uniform size.

   (c) Manually reposition all open apps so that you can see the content of each.

   (d) Fix an app window(s) to either side or the corners of the screen.

3. What phrase is spoken to use Cortana?

   (a) Hey, Cortana

   (b) Wake up, Cortana

   (c) No specific phrase is necessary.

   (d) You cannot speak to Cortana.

4. Apps or programs on the Start menu are represented by rectangular icons known as:

   (a) Gadgets.

   (b) Tiles.

   (c) Thumbnails.

   (d) Boxes.

5. What feature is used to organize and access groups of open windows for different purposes, such as Schoolwork and Entertainment?

   (a) Windows Defender

   (b) Windows desktop

   (c) Virtual desktop

   (d) Task Manager

6. Which of the following best describes the Action Center?

   (a) Removes unnecessary files from the computer

   (b) Includes the clock and other icons that relate to the status or setting of a program

   (c) Contains shortcuts to the most frequently used folders

   (d) Provides status information, notifications, and recommended actions

7. Adding a tile to the Start menu or an icon to the taskbar is known as:

   (a) Snapping.

   (b) Snipping.

   (c) Pinning.

   (d) Tacking.

8. Which of the following is a method of switching between open windows?

   (a) Alt+Tab

   (b) Task View

   (c) Both A and B

   (d) Neither A nor B

9. When you restore down a window, you:

   (a) Keep it open, but remove it from view.

   (b) Make the window smaller, but keep it displayed on the desktop.

   (c) Minimize the window's height but leave its width unchanged.

   (d) Minimize the window's width but leave its height unchanged.

10. When you enter search keywords in the search box of File Explorer and the OneDrive option is selected:

   (a) The search is limited to that specific location.

   (b) The search cannot be further narrowed.

   (c) The search is automatically expanded to include every folder on the hard drive.

   (d) The search is limited to the selected location but can be expanded if you like.

Practice Exercises

1 Investments

FROM SCRATCH

You have some extra funds accumulating in your savings account. You want to begin investing, but before you take the plunge, you decide to watch a few stocks and learn more about them. You also want to take advantage of some Microsoft apps to read more about the stock market and investing, in general. You create and add tiles to a new group on your Start menu and also create a separate desktop for your investment activities, so you can easily come back to all the material. Refer to Figure 1.30 as you complete the exercise.

 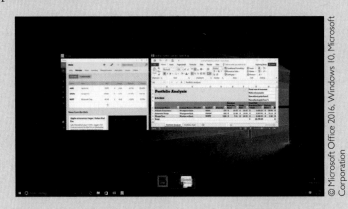

© Microsoft Office 2016, Windows 10, Microsoft Corporation

FIGURE 1.30 Investments Start Menu

a. Open a Blank Word document, and save it as **win01p1Investments_LastFirst**. Minimize the window.

b. Click the **search box**, type **Money**, right-click **Money Trusted Windows Store app** that displays at the top of the results list, and then click **Pin to Start**.

> **TROUBLESHOOTING:** If the Money app is already pinned to start, skip to the next step.

c. Click **Start**, and move the Money tile to a blank area on the Start menu.

d. Point above the Money tile to display the Name group box, click inside the box, type **Investments**, and then press **Enter**.

   You have created a new group.

e. Click **Money**, and then click **Watchlist** from the top menu. Click **Add to Watchlist** (the plus sign), and then type **MSFT**, and press **Enter**. (Note: MSFT might already be added to the Watchlist.) Repeat this step to add **GOOG** and **AAPL**.

> **TROUBLESHOOTING:** If MSFT is the first stock begin added to the Watchlist, click Add a favorite in the middle of the screen..

f. Click **Pin to Start** ⊞ to pin the Watchlist to the Start menu. Click **Close**.

g. Click **MSFT** on the Watchlist, and click **Pin to Start**. Click the **Back arrow**. Repeat for **AAPL**. Minimize Money.

h. Click **Start**, and notice the three new tiles you have added. Drag the three new tiles into the Investments group.

i. Right-click the **Money tile**, and click **Resize**, and then select **Wide**. Resize the Watchlist tile to **Wide**.

j. Drag to arrange the tiles within the Investments group to match the arrangement in Figure 1.30.

k. Press **PrtSc**, click **Word** on the taskbar, and then press **Ctrl+V**. Save the document and minimize Word.

l. Click **Start**, and click the **Watchlist** tile.

m. Open Cortana, click the **Notebook icon**, click **Finance**. In the Stocks you're tracking section, click **GOOG**, and then click the **trashcan icon** to remove GOOG from the Watchlist.

n. Click **Excel** in the Start menu, type **Portfolio Analysis** in the Search for online templates box. Select the template that results, and click **Create**.

o. Click **File**, click **Save As**, click **Browse**, and then click **Documents** in the This PC folder. Check that This PC>Documents displays in the Address bar.

p. Type **win01p1Portfolio_LastFirst** in the File name box, click **New folder**, and name the folder **Portfolio**, click **Open**, and then click **Save**. Minimize Excel.

q. Open **Task View**, click the **plus sign** to create a new desktop, and then drag the Excel and Money thumbnails to Desktop 2.

r. Point to **Desktop 2** to display two thumbnails. Click **PrtSc**, point to **Desktop 1**, click **Word**, press **Enter** twice, and then press **Ctrl+V**. Save the document.

s. Click **X** to delete Desktop 2, and close Excel. Open File Explorer, click **Documents** in the Quick access or This PC section, right-click the **Portfolio folder**, and then click **Pin to Quick access**.

t. Right-click **Portfolio** in the Documents folder and rename it as **Investments**.

Notice that the folder name also changes in Quick access.

u. Press **PrtSc**, click **Word**, press **Enter** twice, and then press **Ctrl+V**. Save the document.

v. Click **Start**, click **Settings**, type **Firewall** in the Find a setting search box, and then click **Windows Firewall**. Click **Turn Windows Firewall on or off**, and then in the Public network settings, click to select **Block all incoming connections, including those in the list of allowed apps**.

w. Press **PrtSc**, click **Word**, press **Enter** twice, and then press **Ctrl+V**. Save the document and minimize Word.

x. Click **Cancel**, close the Windows Firewall window, and then close the Settings window.

y. Save and close the file. Based on your instructor's directions, submit win01p1Investments_LastFirst. Close any other open windows.

2 Planning a Trip

FROM SCRATCH

You and your family want to take a road trip through some National Parks. You volunteer to begin planning. You start by opening the Calendar app to block out the desired week, and then open the Map app to help with the navigation. You pin both apps to the Start menu, and place them in a new group. You also create a new desktop in which to display them. You create a folder and pin it to Quick access, so everyone in the family can easily find the folder and save their ideas. Your friend visited some National Parks last year and sent you her photos in a zipped folder. You move them to the new folder, and then extract the pictures so your family can better access them. You use Disk Cleanup to make sure your computer remains in tip-top shape. Refer to Figure 1.31 as you complete the exercise.

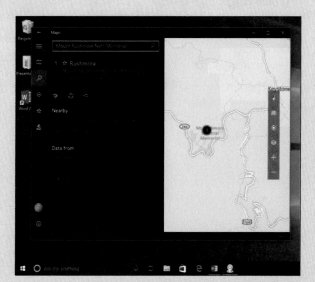

FIGURE 1.31 Planning a Trip

a. Start **Word**, create a **Blank document**, and then save the document as **win01p2Vacation_ LastFirst**. Keep the document open.

b. Click **Start**, click **All apps**, and scroll to find **Calendar**. Right-click and select **Pin to Start**. Note: If Calendar app is already on the Start menu, skip to the next step.

c. Click **Start**, click the **Calendar app**, click **New event**, click in the Event name box, and type **Family Vacation**. Click **Start**, and type **June 01, 2018**. Click **End**, and type **June 14, 2018**. Click to select the **All day box**, click the **Show As: box**, select **Tentative**, click the **Reminder box**, and then select **None**.

> **TROUBLESHOOTING:** If you have never worked with the Calendar app before, you might need to click Welcome, and confirm an email account before working with the application.

d. Press **PrtSc**, click **Word** on the taskbar, and then click inside a blank area of the document. Press **Ctrl+V**, click **Save**, and then minimize Word. Click **Save & Close** on the Calendar app. Close Calendar.

e. Click **Start**, click **All apps**, and scroll to find **Maps**, if it is not already on the Start menu. Right-click and select **Pin to Start**.

f. Open **Maps**, type **Yellowstone National Park**, select the entry in the resulting list, click the **Star** (Add to Favorites), type **Yellowstone** in the Nickname box, and then click **Save**. Repeat for **Grand Teton National Park**, using **Teton** as the Nickname, and **Mount Rushmore National Memorial**, using **Rushmore** as the Nickname.

g. Press **PrtSc**, click **Word**, press **Enter** twice, press **Ctrl+V**, click **Save,** and then minimize the Word document. Close Maps.

h. Open **File Explorer**, click **Documents** (in either This PC or Quick access), and then click **New folder** on the Home tab in the New group. Name the folder **Vacation**. Press **Enter**. Click **Pin to Quick access** in the Clipboard group.

i. Navigate to your student data files, and locate the *win01p2Pictures* zipped folder. Click the zipped folder, press and hold **Ctrl**, and drag it to the Vacation folder you pinned to Quick access.

j. Click **Vacation** in Quick access, click the **win01p2Pictures zipped folder**, click the **Extract tab**, and then click **Extract all**. Click **Extract**.

k. Click **Vacation** in the Address bar, click the **zipped win01p2Pictures folder** in the File list, and then click **Delete**.

l. Double-click to open the **win01p2Pictures folder** so the thumbnail images display in the File list.

m. Press **PrtSc**, click **Word** on the taskbar, press **Enter** twice, press **Ctrl+V**, and then save the Word document. Close all open File Explorer windows.

n. Click the **search box**, type **Disk Cleanup**, and then click **Disk Cleanup Desktop app**.

o. Click **OK** to run Disk Cleanup on the C: drive, and then in the results, click to select **Recycle Bin** and deselect all other check boxes.

p. Press **PrtSc**, click **Word**, press **Enter** twice, press **Ctrl+V**.

q. Save and close the file. Based on your instructor's directions submit win01p2Vacation_LastFirst.

Mid-Level Exercises

1 5K Pound Run

FROM SCRATCH

To satisfy your community outreach graduation requirement, you and a friend have decided to organize a 5K run to benefit the regional animal rescue society. You are responsible for organizing the paperwork and pulling together the details. To start, you use Windows 10 to organize the various apps and files so you can easily find and work with all that you need at any time.

a. Start **Word**, create a **Blank document**, and it save as **win01m1Race_LastFirst**.

b. Type **5K Pound Run**, and press **Enter** twice. Save the file.

c. Pin Word to the taskbar.

d. Locate the Calendar app and Map app in All apps, and pin both to the Start menu.

e. Put the Maps and Calendar apps in a new group on the Start menu, and name the group **5K Race**.

f. Pin the Sticky Notes app to the Start menu, and add it to the 5K Race group.

g. Use PrtSc to capture a screenshot of the Start menu, and paste it in the win01m1Race_LastFirst document.

h. Use the search box to find information on the Web about 5K races in your area in April. Click any link that displays a list of races. Take a screenshot of the Web results, copy and paste to the Word document.

i. Open File Explorer, create a new folder where you save your student files named **5KPoundRun**, and then pin the folder to Quick access.

j. Create subfolders in the 5KPoundRun folder, and name them: **Sponsors**, **Permissions**, **Promotions**, **Registration**, and **Follow-Up**. Rename the Registration folder to **Participants**.

k. Click **Word** on the taskbar, click **File**, and then click **New**. Type **Seasonal Event Flyer (Spring)** in the templates search box. Click **Create**, and then save to the Promotions folder as **win01m1Flyer_LastFirst**.

 DISCOVER

l. Add the tag **5KPound Run** to win01m1Flyer_LastFirst. Take a screenshot to show the tag, copy and paste to the win01m1Race_LastFirst document. Save the flyer.

m. Create a new virtual desktop (Desktop 2), and drag the flyer into Desktop 2 in Task View. Display the contents of Desktop 2, and then take a screenshot and paste the screenshot into win01m1Race_LastFirst.

n. Compress the 5KPoundRun folder and rename it **win01m1PoundRun_LastFirst**.

o. Open the Action Center. Take a screenshot of the Action Center. Paste the screenshot into win01m1Race_LastFirst.

p. Save and close the file. Based on your instructor's directions, submit win01m1Race_LastFirst and win01m1PoundRun_LastFirst.

2 Junk Business

FROM SCRATCH

You and a college friend were asked to reconfigure some old computers for an inner city after school club. Because you had a few spare parts and some hardware expertise, you rebuilt several computers and installed Windows 10. Now you will check the system of each computer to verify that it is workable and configured correctly. Assume the computer you are working on to complete this exercise is the computer you rebuilt.

a. Open Word, create a Blank document, and save the file as **win01m2Junk_LastFirst**. Snap Word to the left side of your screen.

b. Open the Action Center. Press **PrtSc** to capture a screen image of the Action Center. In Word, type **Step b:**. Press **Enter**, and then press **Ctrl+V** to paste the screen. Underneath the image, describe any Notifications that display. Save the document. Close the Action Center.

c. Type **Resource Monitor** in the search box. Pin Resource Monitor to the Start menu. Open Resource Monitor, and click the **Memory tab**. Snap the Resource Monitor window to the right side of your screen. Click **Word** on the taskbar, press **Enter** twice, type **Step c:**, press **Enter**, and then list the amount of memory *In Use*, *Standby*, *Free*, and *Installed*. Add a sentence that comments on whether the amount of memory in the system seems sufficient. Close the Resource Monitor. Save the Word document.

d. Pin Disk Cleanup to the Start menu. Type **Windows Accessories** as a new group name, in the Start menu, and drag **Disk Cleanup** and **Resource Monitor** to the group. Take a screenshot of the Start menu, open Word, type **Step d:**, and then paste the screenshot.

e. Open File Explorer, and create a new folder in Documents named Client Invoices. Pin the Client Invoices folder to Quick access, and then open the Client Invoices folder. Take a screenshot of File Explorer, open Word, type **Step e:**, and then paste the screenshot.

f. Save and close the file. Based on your instructor's directions, submit win01m2Junk_LastFirst.

Beyond the Classroom

Speech Class Notes

For your speech class, you must develop a speech that teaches how to do something. Because Windows 10 is a relatively new operating system, you decide to demonstrate some of its features. You will use Word to record a few notes that will help you make your presentation. After completing your notes, save the document as **win01b1Speech_LastFirst**. Listing your points in numerical order, provide directions to the class on the following:

- Customize the Start menu.
- Pin programs to the taskbar and the Start menu.
- Use the search box to find and open a program that you think is installed on your computer and to get help on an item related to Windows 10.
- Use Cortana.
- Use the Action Center.

Based on your instructor's directions, submit win01b1Speech_LastFirst.

Computer Security Report

DISASTER
RECOVERY

You depend on a laptop computer for most of what you do and you would be lost should you lose your laptop or the data and programs on it. A recent scare, when you temporarily misplaced the laptop, has led you to consider precautions you can take to make sure your computer and its data are protected. You will use the search box and Cortana to explore some suggestions for protecting your laptop. Create a report that describes how you would secure your laptop and the data, programs, and personal information on your laptop against harm. Consider virus protection software, cloud storage options, backup and recovery software and hardware, and ways to protect and secure your hardware. Use Word to record the report, save the report as **win01b2Protection_LastFirst**, and submit as directed by your instructor.

Capstone Exercise

For your Entrepreneurial class, BUS401, you are planning a new business as the ongoing project. Since you will be working with many of the same apps and documents throughout the semester, you decide to use many of the new Windows 10 features to help you stay organized and be as efficient as possible.

Work with the Start Menu

To start things off, you want to pin a few apps to the Start menu that you know you will be working with consistently throughout the semester. You will put them in a group and give the group a meaningful name.

a. Open a new Word document and save it as **win01c1Business_LastFirst**.

b. Locate and pin to the Start menu, the Calculator app, the Snipping Tool, Word 2016, and Excel 2016.

c. Pin Word 2016 and the Snipping Tool to the taskbar.

d. Create a new group on the Start menu, name it **Business Apps**, and move the apps you added to the Start menu in Step b to this group.

e. Resize the Calculator app and the Snipping Tool tiles to Small. Keep Word 2016 and Excel 2016 tiles to Medium. Arrange the tiles so the Word and Excel tiles are next to each other, and the Calculator and Snipping Tool tiles are below the Word and Excel tiles.

f. Take a screenshot of the Start menu. Paste the screenshot to win01c1Business_LastFirst.

Use Task View and Virtual Desktops

There are a few Excel and Word files that you will be using for this project. So that you can get to them easily, you put them onto a separate desktop.

a. Open Word and search for a Business Plan template. Select the first template, named Business plan. Create and save the document as **win01c1BusinessPlan_LastFirst**.

b. Open Excel and search for a Profit and Loss template. Select the first template, named Profit and Loss Statement. Save the workbook as **win01c1ProfitLoss_LastFirst**.

c. Create a new virtual desktop (Desktop 2) and drag the Excel and Word files created in Steps a and b above to Desktop 2. Keep win01c1Business_LastFirst in Desktop 1.

d. Display Desktop 2, and snap the Word document to the left and the Excel workbook to the right of the screen and take a screenshot.

e. Display Desktop 1, and paste the screenshot to win01c1Business_LastFirst.

Use Cortana and the Search Box

One of the first things you need to do for your business is to write a Mission Statement. You use the search box to find information on Mission Statements, and then use Cortana to set up a reminder for you to talk to your professor about this, as well.

a. Type **how to write a mission statement** in the search box. Open the Entrepreneur.com link (or a similar link). Drag the browser window to Desktop 2.

b. Display Desktop 2, and then using the Windows and arrow keys, snap the browser window to the lower left corner, and the Word window to the upper left corner.

c. Use Cortana in Desktop 2 to add a reminder to meet with your professor. Choose a day and time next week.

d. Take a screenshot of Desktop 2 and Cortana Reminders. Display Desktop 1, and paste the screenshot to win01c1Business_LastFirst.

e. Close all windows in Desktop 2.

Use File Explorer

Although using virtual desktops helps to organize your active documents, you want to create a good file management structure so all your Entrepreneurial class documents are in one place and easy to access throughout the semester. You use File Explorer to create folders and pin one folder to Quick access.

a. Open File Explorer, and then open the Documents folder in This PC. Create a new folder named **BUS401**. Pin this folder to Quick access.

b. Open the BUS401 folder, and create three new folders named **Business Plan Documents**, **Financial Statements**, and **Marketing Info**.

c. Take a screenshot of File Explorer and paste the screenshot to win01c1Business_LastFirst.

Work with Files and Folders

With the new folder structure set up, you reorganize your existing files. You then compress the BUS401 folder so you can more easily share it with your professor and others.

a. Save the win01c1ProfitLoss_LastFirst workbook to the Financial Statements folder, and move win01c1BusinessPlan_LastFirst to the Business Plan Documents folder.

b. Compress the BUS401 folder, and rename the folder **win01c1BUS401_LastFirst**.

Use the Action Center and Administrative Tools

One of the other components of the BUS401 project is to create a marketing video. You know creating and editing a video uses lots of computer processing and memory, so you check the status of your system resources to see if this will be the best computer to use going forward. You also want to check the Action Center for any new notifications.

a. Open Resource Monitor. Click the **Memory tab**, use the Snipping Tool to take a Rectangular Snip of the Resource Monitor window, and then paste it into win01c1Business_LastFirst.

b. Click the **CPU tab**, and then use the Snipping Tool to take a Rectangular Snip of the Resource Monitor window and paste it into win01c1Business_LastFirst. Close the Resource Monitor.

c. Open the Action Center. Take a screenshot, and then paste the screenshot in to win01c1Business_LastFirst.

d. Save and close the document. Based on your instructor's directions, submit win01c1Business_LastFirst and win01c1BUS401_LastFirst.

Glossary

Action center A location in Windows 10, accessed by an icon in the Notifications area on the taskbar, that provides status information, notifications, and recommended actions for various maintenance and security settings.

Compressed (zipped) folder A folder created with the Zip feature, contains a file or group of files. A compressed folder uses less drive space and can be transferred or shared with other users more quickly.

Cortana Microsoft 10's personal assistant that helps search the Web and your PC, and can also assist with reminders, tasks, and other activities.

Desktop The primary working area of Windows 10 that contains objects such as windows and icons.

Disk Cleanup An administrative tool in Windows that is used to remove unnecessary files from the computer.

File Explorer The Windows app that is used to create folders and manage files and folders across various storage locations.

File History A utility in Windows that continuously makes copies of your important files so that you can recover them if you encounter a file problem.

File management The means of providing an organizational structure to file and folders.

Firewall A software program included in Windows 10 that helps to product against unauthorized access, or hacking, to your computer.

Icon A graphical link to a program, file, folder, or other item related to your computer.

Jump List List of program-specific shortcuts to recently opened files, the program name, an option to pin or unpin the program, and a close window option.

Notification area On the far right of the taskbar, includes the clock and a group of icons that relate to the status of a setting or program.

OneDrive Microsoft's cloud storage system. Saving files to OneDrive enables them to sync across all Windows devices and to be accessible from any Internet-connected device.

Pin A process to add a tile to the Start menu or icon to the taskbar.

Quick access A component of File Explorer that contains shortcuts to the most frequently used folders. Folders can be pinned and removed from Quick access.

Recycle Bin Temporary storage for files deleted from the computer's hard drive or OneDrive.

Resource Monitor A feature that displays how the computer is using its key resources such as the CPU and RAM.

Search box A feature located on the taskbar. Combined with Cortana, or used alone, it provides a convenient way to search your computer or the Web.

Shortcut An icon on the desktop designated with a small arrow in the bottom-left corner, that provides a link a program.

Sleep A power saving state that puts work and settings in memory and draws a small amount of power to allow the computer to resume full-power operation quickly.

Snip A screenshot taken with the Snipping Tool accessory application in Windows.

Start menu A feature that provides the main access to all programs on your computer.

Task Manager A tool that displays the programs and processes that are running on your computer. It is also used to close a non-responding program.

Task view A button on the taskbar that enables the user to view thumbnail previews of all open tasks in one glance.

Taskbar The horizontal bar at the bottom of the desktop that displays open applications, the Notification area, the Search box, and pinned apps or programs.

Tile A rectangular icon on the Start menu that allow you to access programs and apps.

Title bar The long bar at the top of each window that displays the name of the folder, file, or program displayed in the open window.

Virtual desktop A way to organize and access groups of windows for different purposes.

Windows app A program that displays full screen without any borders or many controls. It is designed to be best viewed and used on smaller screens such as those on smartphone and tablets.

Windows Defender Antispyware and antivirus software included in Windows 10.

Windows Update A utility in Windows that provides a means to initiate updates and modifications pushed to the user that enhances Windows security or fixes problems.

Index

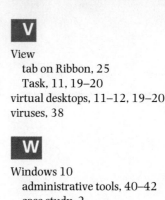